How to have
hard conversations
at work

smart conflict

Alice Driscoll and
Louise van Haarst

First published in Great Britain by Practical Inspiration Publishing, 2025

ISBN (9781788606578) (paperback)
(9781788606561) (hardback)
(9781788606592) (ebook)

EU GPSR representative: LOGOS EUROPE, 9 rue Nicolas Poussin, LA ROCHELLE 17000, France Contact@logoseurope.eu

Want to bulk-buy copies of this book for your team and colleagues? We can customize the content and co-brand *Smart Conflict: How to have hard conversations at work* to suit your business's needs.

Please email info@practicalinspiration.com for more details.

"This is such an important book for anyone in the workplace. Conflict is often seen as taboo in an office environment but the right kind of conflict leads to progress. *Smart Conflict* helps leaders ensure this uncomfortable topic becomes easier to embrace and manage."

Charlie Rudd,
Group Chief Executive Officer, Publicis Groupe

"Working closely with Founders operating in fast-moving environments of innovation and change, I've learned that conflict is not only inevitable, it's essential. But too often, conflict is either ignored or mishandled, leading to missed opportunities for growth and transformation. *Smart Conflict* is the most insightful and practical resource I've found for navigating the reality of everyday conflict in the workplace. It offers a powerful framework for having the difficult conversations we tend to avoid, along with transformative reframes, deep insights, and actionable tools. This book doesn't just explain conflict - it equips you to handle it with clarity, transparency, and confidence. You can put it to use immediately."

Eleanor Ford,
Chief People Officer, Zinc VC

"*Smart Conflict* is a brilliantly practical playbook for anyone trying to build a culture of high support and high challenge. Hard conversations are essential and this book helps you get them right. As someone short on time, I love that it's structured for busy people, so you can find what you need when you need it. A book I know I'll return to often."

Rebecca Passmore,
Group Chief Operating Officer, PureGym

"*Smart Conflict* is a timely, evidence-based guide for leaders seeking to build the elusive high-performing culture. With practical tools at every step the book is an essential read for every manager in today's world of work".

Professor Jonathan Passmore,
Henley Business School, UK & Senior Vice
President, EZRA Coaching, LHH

"In sales – and in leadership – the conversations we avoid often cost us the most. *Smart Conflict* delivers a practical, actionable framework for tackling the tough discussions that drive trust, performance, and results. We need to build cultures where candor and accountability go hand in hand, and this book is helping us get there faster."

Michael Roughsedge,
Global Chief Sales Officer, Avanade

"This is a brilliant reminder of why avoiding conflict in business is often a bad idea. *Smart Conflict* is refreshing, uplifting, and most of all incredibly helpful. More than a book about handling conflict, it is a practical guide to embracing it. If I wanted to unlock the creativity and productivity of any team, I'd recommend that they all read this."

Oli Barrett MBE,
Serial Co-Founder and Presenter

"Smart Conflict is grounded in the latest research, packed with practical tools, and is refreshingly readable. It's a must-read for every leader who wants to build high-performing collaborative teams that can share uncomfortable truths effectively."

Vinay Abrol,
Chief Operating Officer, Liontrust Asset Management PLC

"Conflicts within teams are inevitable when people work together but they don't have to be destructive. The key isn't in the avoidance of conflict; it's managing it in ways that build trust rather than erode it. Smart Conflict is the essential guide for organizations and team members dedicated to fostering courageous conversations, where hard truths are spoken with respect and purpose. This book equips leaders and team members alike with practical tools to transform difficult discussions into opportunities for innovation, inclusion, and growth. For teams ready to approach conflicts with courage and clarity, *Smart Conflict* is here to help."

Teik Ngan Loy,
Chairman at Taylor's Education Group, Malaysia

"In fashion, where creativity, pace and pressure constantly intersect, navigating relationships can be as complex as the work itself. *Smart Conflict* offers a rare combination of emotional intelligence and practical strategy, supporting leaders to approach difficult moments with clarity, composure and confidence. The Five R model blends insight and empathy in a way that is both empowering and actionable. This book is not just about managing conflict; it's about transforming it into a leadership strength. Clear, considered and deeply reassuring, it's a timely resource for building stronger, more resilient teams."

Claire Hillard,
Group Senior Sustainability Manager,
Selfridges Group

"This is the kind of book that if it had been published 50 years ago, we might have a lot fewer problems in the world. Inhale this book and you will become highly skilled in navigating workplace conflict."

Ben Keene,
Co-Founder, Rebel Book Club & Raaise

"Reading this book is a real lightbulb moment - whether you're an experienced business leader or just beginning your career. It explains why so many of those professional interactions we chalk up as having gone badly, been uncomfortable or due to a "personality clash" result from unclear communication and poor conflict management. Exploring this hugely practical and relatable guide to hard conversations will genuinely change how you communicate for the better. It's by no means easy but it's definitely empowering."

Melanie Hayes,
Managing Partner, Bethnal Green Ventures

"As a Leader, reading this book has enabled me to step back and reflect on how I respond in difficult moments and how I want my team and our organisational culture to engage in tough conversations. *Smart Conflict* explores why we need to facilitate healthy conflict at work, as well as all the societal and personal factors that may be hindering us from doing so. It is a practical guide but also incredibly rich in context; it has genuinely inspired me to take steps to approach things differently."

Naomi Pohl,
General Secretary, The Musicians' Union

"I love this book! In my role as a CEO of a charity, I consume a lot of books, podcasts, articles relating to leadership and management which will often have a focus on workplace relations and conflict. While I can often find something useful from these, I am equally often left feeling that the author has never worked in a real organisation in their lives, or at least not for a long time. What I really appreciate about this book is that Louise and Alice have clearly had interesting careers in which they have personally dealt with the challenges and joy that workplaces can bring. They combine this experience with a depth and breadth of knowledge and expertise that jumps out on every page. They pull together so many threads of evidence across psychology, leadership, psychotherapy, management as well as their own work in coaching to build a compelling set of principles to underpin the most critical and yet often hardest part of any workplace – the relationships within them."

Rebecca Gill,
Chief Executive Officer, ROSA

"Today's world is full of conflict, whether in our personal or business lives. This book is packed with techniques, tools, and case-studies that Alice & Louise use to help you navigate more effectively the conflicts we face every day. It helps you handle more successfully those difficult conversations we all hate to have. It helps turn destructive, negative, and sometimes nasty conflict situations into positive healthy ones. Put simply *Smart Conflict* is a masterclass in how to tackle conflict well. It is a must have in any good leader's toolkit."

Andy Hassoon,
Chief Executive Officer, CTO Craft

"This book is an invaluable resource for anyone seeking practical, actionable strategies to navigate and resolve tensions in professional settings. It is clear that Alice and Louise are accomplished conflict specialists as the book combines deep expertise and personal experience with real-world insights, making it both accessible and impactful. Their guidance is not only practical and transformative, but it also has a warmth to it that most professional development books lack. A must-read for leaders and professionals at every level."

Sarah Wigington,
Head of Corporate, International Law Firm

Smart

/smart/

1) Intelligent, or able to think quickly or intelligently in difficult situations.
2) Showing good judgement.

Conflict

/ˈkɒnflɪkt/

1) A serious disagreement or argument, typically a protracted one.
2) An active disagreement between people with opposing opinions or principles.
3) Be incompatible or at variance; clash.
4) A state of discord caused by the actual or perceived opposition of need, values, and interests.

For Isadora, Raphael and Sylvie, my greatest teachers.
And for Ivo, for always being on my team – LvH

For my children, Florence and Bertie. And for Christian,
for making hard conversations safe at last – AD

Contents

Introduction

The quality of your life is defined
by the quality of your conflict.

We – Louise and Alice – came to be fascinated with conflict at work because in our early careers – in our own different and unique ways – we were both *terrible* at it.

We met while studying for a Masters in Coaching and Behaviour Change at business school, both pursuing a career pivot after 20 years' experience in our respective industries. Louise had worked as a management consultant and change specialist in the International NGO and UK voluntary sectors, and Alice had been in the leadership teams of several UK advertising agencies before joining and growing a healthtech startup. Coincidentally, we had both taken a brief foray into different types of entrepreneurship and the startup world before realizing our true passions lay in people development. When we met we were already running our own separate Executive and Leadership Team Coaching practices and over many conversations, group supervisions, shared workshops, lunches (and maybe a few glasses of wine) we realized that we were – again, in our different and unique ways – increasingly working with clients whose primary presenting issue was some kind of workplace conflict. And we realized that if we combined the approaches we were using separately, the two halves could come together to make a comprehensive and powerful whole methodology, one which would eventually become Smart Conflict.

But first, back to being terrible at conflict at work.

As we'll explain later using our Default Conflict Styles Model, we could say that there are two extremes when it comes to default adult conflict style – Avoidant and Aggressive. The conditions that create our default settings when it comes to conflict will comprise a mix of genetics, the norms of our family of origin, our cultural influences, and our lifetime experiences of relational conflict, the good and the bad.

As we got to know each other better, we learned that growing up – and even though we are both from culturally similar and geographically close parts of England – our experiences of conflict in our families of origin were at the opposite ends of the scale. While Alice grew up in a house where hearts were worn on sleeves, frustrations were aired, and feelings were felt out loud, Louise grew up in a house where (in almost 35 years of marriage) her parents never argued, but where – at times – you could have cut the atmosphere with a knife.

We've often mused on the roles we instinctively took as children of those families – Alice the peacemaker intent on smoothing things over, and Louise the truth-teller, pointing out the elephant in the room whether it was welcome or not (it usually wasn't). We can all reflect on the effect that our early experiences have had on our adult 'settings' (this is an exercise we'll invite you to undertake in the *Reflection* chapter), and it doesn't take too much of a stretch to see how these childhood experiences might have formed the people we became at work once we took our first full-time jobs in our twenties – for better or worse.

While it's undeniable we were high performers in our respective roles, we both struggled with workplace conflict in different ways. As Louise discovered, even in a robust campaigning culture, the role of truth-teller isn't always welcomed (especially when that truth is seen only from one perspective – your own). One person's value-driven guardian-of-what's-right is another person's self-righteous, overconfident pain in the backside. Not a great look. And not a great way of convincing anyone of your point of view, however meritorious it might be.

Alice, who began her graduate working life in the cut-and-thrust of adland in the early 2000s, found herself surrounded by strong, bolshy characters with fixed views and seemingly free-range permission to rant and rage up and down the corridors at anyone who had the misfortune to cross their paths. Reduced to tears on many occasions from being in the wrong place at the wrong time, she regularly found herself ricocheting between being frozen with fear one moment, and being swept along in the current of the aggressive, alpha culture the next.

In her book *Insight*, organizational psychologist Dr. Tasha Eurich explains that unless we take steps to improve our self-awareness (an understanding both of who we are on the inside and – critically – how others see us on the outside), we can end up having what she calls an unwelcome 'alarm clock moment'[1] when we are unavoidably introduced to how people are experiencing our behaviour, often when it is too late to do anything about it. It's the unexpected negative feedback in our performance review, the exasperated harsh words from the team member who's had enough, the out-of-the-blue firing.

We've both had our own painful alarm clock moments with conflict at work. One of us being adeptly and – in hindsight – deservedly, managed out of a role where her increasing commitment to not-suffering-fools-gladly had become pretty unpleasant for everyone. The other exploding like a coiled spring when she could no longer hold down the pressure and resentment she felt for feeling set up to fail on a project. We'll protect the innocent by not saying who was who, but if you catch us at an unguarded moment, we might share.

Sometimes an emotionally painful experience is the only way we learn the consequences of our 'default' behaviour. In writing this book our intention is to save you that pain by learning the skills you need to have hard conversations with calm, confidence, compassion and credibility – and crucially with the self-awareness that drives real growth.

We'd hope that now, in our forties, with many years of work experience, coach-training, client successes and personal development work behind us, we are very different and much more evolved people to those emotional and un-self-aware twenty-somethings (ok, maybe even thirty-somethings). It's also our hope that by making and learning from our own mistakes the hard way, and helping our clients to navigate theirs, we can help you avoid making your own and feel that bit smarter next time you encounter a moment of conflict at work.

Why does conflict at work matter?

> *'Peace is not the absence of conflict, but the ability to cope with it'* – Dorothy Thompson[2]

Relational conflict is an inevitable part of life. And it's universal. Most people instinctively feel like it's something to be avoided. Some people will go to extreme lengths to do so. There are others who enjoy the cut and thrust of a heated conversation and can easily brush it off. And a few who barely register something as an intense conflict while the other person feels like they've emotionally gone 20 rounds. Most of us sit somewhere in the middle of that spectrum – we'd prefer to avoid hard conversations but know there are times we need to have them, doing our best to get them over with quickly and trying not to have the whole thing blow up in our faces.

Conflict is also an inevitable part of work. Done well, it can be a catalyst for innovation, collaboration and inclusion. On the outside, it looks like healthy debate and constructive challenge. On the inside, it feels productive and energizing. It fosters strong relationships and self-awareness. It helps us grow individually and collectively. Done badly (and it often *is* done badly) it can be a toxic, destructive force that dominates team culture, negatively impacts employee well-being, and destroys value. It might sound counterintuitive, but workplaces with too little conflict – where the big issues are politely ignored, and everyone elegantly dances round the latest elephant in the room – are just as problematic as those where voices are raised, and the candour is by far *too* radical.

It's our belief that the ability to manage conflict at work well is the most underrated professional skill of all, but it's one that's rarely given attention or investment in corporate learning and development programmes at any career stage, from graduate to senior leadership. This is perplexing to us, but also what fundamentally inspires us in our mission to upskill generations of current and future leaders across industries with these powerful, simple, but counterintuitive techniques.

If you are skilled at handling conflict at work, the impact can be professionally and personally transformational. However, the costs of getting it wrong can be shockingly high. Research is remarkably consistent in finding that conflict in teams can reduce overall performance by up to 22%, especially when unresolved task conflicts (i.e. simple disagreements about what or how things are done) escalate into interpersonal issues that create difficult dynamics.[3] According to a 2022 report from the Advisory, Conciliation and Arbitration Service (Acas), on average employees spend 2.8 hours per week dealing with conflict, translating into a productivity loss of approximately £28.5 billion annually in the UK,[4] whilst the Society for Human Resource Management (SHRM) estimates a productivity loss and absenteeism cost of $2.1 billion per day in the US as a direct result of incivility in the workplace.[5] Companies spend untold millions on clever new initiatives that might see a 1% performance uplift against one measure or another, while leaving on the table the potential 22% gain achievable if they can learn how to embrace debate, resolve differences and have hard but necessary conversations well.[6]

But the business impact doesn't tell the personal story. Being in unhealthy conflict frequently over a sustained period can be extremely damaging to mental health, with employees who experience workplace conflict reporting higher stress levels.[7] Prolonged exposure to relational conflict also correlates with a higher likelihood of developing anxiety or depression.[8] And the effects can be enduring – a number of studies conclude that unresolved workplace conflicts are a major predictor of long-term psychological distress, months or even years later.[9,10]

Yet, most of us will never have a single minute of training or education on the topic. Our working lives thrive or founder according to the strength of the relationships we build with our colleagues, our bosses and the people we manage. And relationships *are* built (as well as broken) through the words and gestures we use in the hundreds of tiny interactions we have each day. In spite of this, often we rely on turning up and hoping for the best, without giving the quality of the relationship or our role in creating it much thought.

However, we can all learn to be strategic – or in our words *smart* – in how we approach conflict at work. With some new tools we can transform how we have hard conversations to create the conditions for high performance, and that builds relationships rather than breaks them. The ability to manage our emotions and communicate well are essential to almost every job we can think of. They are especially essential if you have any kind of leadership ambition. The ability to build respectful, effective relationships with others – even if they see things very differently to you – is incredibly powerful and will take you a long way, at work and in life. In the era of increasingly rapid automation by Artificial Intelligence, excellent human skills have never been more of a differentiator in a competitive employment landscape. More reason than ever (if you needed it) to get good at handling conflict, and fast.

Why did we write this book?

Together we lead The Power House, a global consultancy offering leadership coaching and development, organizational culture transformation and education and training in Smart Conflict. We also provide hands-on de-escalation of workplace conflicts using our *Conflict Wayfinder* methodology – a unique blend of coaching, mediation, and Smart Conflict techniques.

We wrote this book because we were so often being asked by clients for recommendations of a resource that contained the tools and techniques we teach, and, while there are a few that address aspects of how to have hard conversations well, try as we might we could never find one that fit the bill. So, we've written the book that our clients were asking for, and the one we wish that someone had put into our hands while we were struggling with hard conversations at work in our earlier careers. Over thousands of hours of one-to-one coaching, team coaching, group workshops and masterclasses we've learned what does and doesn't work for our clients, discovered what creates positive culture shifts for organizations, and honed our unique approach.

Who is this book for?

This book is for anyone who wants to improve how they navigate hard conversations and conflict at work, whether you are just starting out in your first real job or already a seasoned C-Suite leader (or anything in between).

You may have been told by someone you need to get better at handling conflict (through feedback, a formal performance review or a brush with HR).

You may harbour a fear (or just a suspicion) that you're bad at managing any kind of conflict at work, and simply need to improve this aspect of your communication toolkit.

You might be increasingly frustrated by the lack of healthy challenge in your team and want to learn the tools to upskill yourself and your people to challenge each other more confidently and effectively.

Or you might be concerned about destructive relational conflicts between particular individuals negatively impacting team and business performance and want tools to help fix this.

Wherever you are on the road to becoming conflict competent – this book is for you. Using our Smart Conflict Five R model you will learn new mindsets, tools and techniques to help you build on the skills you already have and learn the sometimes counterintuitive new reflexes you need to create.

Before you start, above all – have hope

The most common thing people say when we mention we're conflict coaches (after they say, 'who knew *that* was a real job?') is:

'I'm terrible with conflict.'

Followed by:

'I really wish you'd come in and talk to my company about handling conflict.'

(The third most common is 'I wish you'd come and teach these skills to my family' but that's outside the scope of this book! Maybe in the next one.)

Very few of us are 'good' with conflict. Most of us are simply nice people who don't want to upset others. Nice people who can get blindsided by a hard conversation we weren't expecting, or that escalated (or flopped) in a way we couldn't have anticipated, leading us to behave in a way that didn't represent our best professional selves. If you are struggling to have hard conversations at work, or involved in some kind of conflict with a colleague that is having a negative impact on you – please have hope. Conflicts can improve and, in most cases, be repaired. You can learn the skills to become confident, competent and, with practice, even masterful at managing the most difficult moments at work with calm, with professionalism, and with a plan.

Hear us when we say – in our experience, and with a little knowhow, it'll all be ok.

What do we mean when we talk about damaging workplace conflict?

'Workplace conflict' is a broad term in common parlance and is usually used to imply the damaging kind. It can include everything from a slightly snappy exchange with a colleague, to a full-on shouting match. It covers the cold war of workmates who openly refuse to speak to each other or work together, to the polite-on-the-surface yet simmering tension of a resentment that has never been discussed. It can be momentary or sustained. It can grow to involve whole teams, or remain an individual, internalized experience, where one person harbours a grudge that everyone else remains in blissful ignorance of (yes, we're sorry to tell you that you can be involved in a workplace conflict you don't even know about).

Damaging workplace conflicts happen between peers in the same team; those who need to work together on a matrixed project; between managers and their direct reports; between co-founders; and within (and between) executive teams and boards. Once we've been in the world of work a while, we'll all have our stories of the people who can't stand each other, the manager who loses their cool as soon as the pressure is on, the subtle undermining or factionalism that happens within a particular team, or the open back-stabbing we've witnessed.

Most conflict at work sits on the lower end of the scale. The majority of adults know what behaviour is and isn't acceptable to stay on the right side of HR and keep clear of any potential disciplinary action, no matter how satisfying it might be to fantasize about a Hollywood movie moment when you *really* 'let them have it.' That said, low level conflict can still spell death by a thousand cuts, and progress into something which feels unmanageable and irreversible. It can create misery and destroy productivity. The good news is that – in almost all cases – with positive intent and a bit of know-how – it can be solved.

What do we mean by Healthy Conflict?

The concept of Healthy Conflict might sound like a total contradiction and there are some that argue with the term, but we stand by it. Some level of conflict, by one definition from the Cambridge Dictionary '*active disagreement between people with opposing opinions or principles*'[11] is a necessary condition of effective debate, innovation and collaboration.

Too little Healthy Conflict at work can be just as damaging to performance as too much Damaging Conflict. Imagine a meeting where everyone is simply nodding along, falling over themselves to agree with the dominant person in the room (be honest, we've all been in that meeting). It might look agreeable, it might feel easy, and it might get the meeting over quickly – but are those really the conditions for smart decisions and cutting-edge-thinking? Probably not. It's more likely a recipe for group-think and stagnation. The chances are half the participants will leave thinking that the wrong decision has been made, or that there's a better way of doing something that no one mentioned.

The highest performing teams do Healthy Conflict well. They share a high enough level of psychological safety to share their ideas, to challenge the thinking of others, to bring new information into the conversation and to speak up when they disagree with something or someone, even when that person is 'the boss.'[12] These are teams where there is high support alongside high challenge. Instead of Relational Conflict ('me against you') they are adept at Task Conflict ('me and you against the problem'). Our Smart Conflict Five R model is informed in large part from observing what these high-performing teams and the individuals in them do well in terms of their *behaviours*, not just the words they use at crunch moments.

What do we mean by hard conversations?

Whether you've just started an apprenticeship or are the chairman of the board, there are times where you are going to have to have hard conversations at work to be able to get what you need from others, resolve difficulties or deliver important but uncomfortable information or news. There can be times when it's right to delegate or defer to others to do the talking. But there will be many moments in your working life where it has to be you.

In our practice we've discovered that within the hundreds of different scenarios clients bring into workplace coaching there are at heart seven categories of common hard conversations people struggle with most:

Feedback conversations – including giving and receiving formal and informal performance feedback, and giving unsolicited feedback on someone's behaviour towards you or others.

Progression conversations – including asking for promotion or pay rise, discussing a lack of expected progression, and telling someone they are not going to be promoted.

Negotiation conversations – including negotiations over money, role or task, and agreeing who is going to do what, and when.

Problem-based conversations – including communicating news about a project or task, deciding on a course of action, and collaborating on solutions.

Decision-making conversations – including how to decide on a course of action, managing opposing viewpoints on decisions, and gaining commitment to action.

Unexpected conversations – including giving or receiving bad news, handling someone's unexpected strong emotions (yours or others'), and responding to a situation when you don't have an answer.

Ending conversations – including resignation, redundancy, firing or reassignment of roles.

In Part 2 of this book we take a deep dive into our Smart Conflict Five R model, which you can use to help you to prepare for, manage and move forward from almost any hard conversation. In the *Readiness* chapter we'll introduce you to our Five-Step Hard Conversations Framework which shows you how to set yourself up for success.

1

What is Smart Conflict?

We spent a long time wrestling over what to call our methodology – *good conflict*, *constructive conflict* and *productive conflict* all do a pretty good job and express elements of our approach, but none sums up quite what we are aiming to help you as reader and human to do. We settled on Smart Conflict as our methodology aims to help you to think quickly and intelligently about hard conversations, and to use your professional judgement to respond – not react – to get to the best possible outcome, and foster a better relationship with the other person *even* if you've both found it difficult.

What is smart about our approach?

We developed Smart Conflict (shown in Figure 1) based on our real-world leadership coaching practice and the thousands of hours we have spent working with individuals and teams helping them to manage their own conflicts. We've drawn on the latest evidence base alongside the most tried-and-tested techniques and smart thinking from group and couples therapy, mediation, team coaching and the science of behaviour change. We've synthesized all this into our own original resources and frameworks to share with you in this book.

Smart Conflict consists of *The Five Rs*:

Reflection – creating awareness of your own conflict 'settings' and reactions.

Regulation – knowing how to check in on how you feel (your state) and calm yourself before, during and after a hard conversation.

Readiness – learning how to prepare effectively and choose the best strategy for a potentially hard conversation and to land your message clearly.

Response – developing techniques to be ready to respond (not react) to the unexpected in the moment.

Repair – understanding the critical importance of repairing relationships after a conflict or hard conversation, and how to do it.

Even mastering one or two of these will make a big difference to how you respond to conflict. However, together The Smart Conflict Five Rs provide a model for preparing for, managing and recovering from conflict and hard conversations at work that can be transformational, both for you personally and for those around you. The secret to being smart isn't to try everything at once; it's about knowing what to tackle first. For centuries, doctors and other medical professionals have used a principle called *triage* – using a set of diagnostics, observations and other criteria to ensure that the most critical patients are treated first, while less urgent cases are handled as resources allow. At its core, triage is the practice of sorting and prioritizing – a structured way to decide what needs immediate attention, what can wait and what isn't worth your energy at all. You can apply this principle to apply Smart Conflict at work. Each of the Five Rs addresses a different aspect of navigating conflict. As you become more familiar with the framework you will begin to instinctively develop a sense of what you need to attend to first, and which steps to take after that.

One of the things we often hear when training and coaching in Smart Conflict is that this all sounds like *a lot of work*. We often hear versions of '*Can't I just go in and tell them straight? All these niceties and preparations sound very time consuming.*' And, well, of course you can – the choice is yours. But you might not always (or even often) get the result you need. And it might cost you a lot more time down the line, trying to resolve and unpick where cross words or misunderstandings have led to bad feeling and things going wrong.

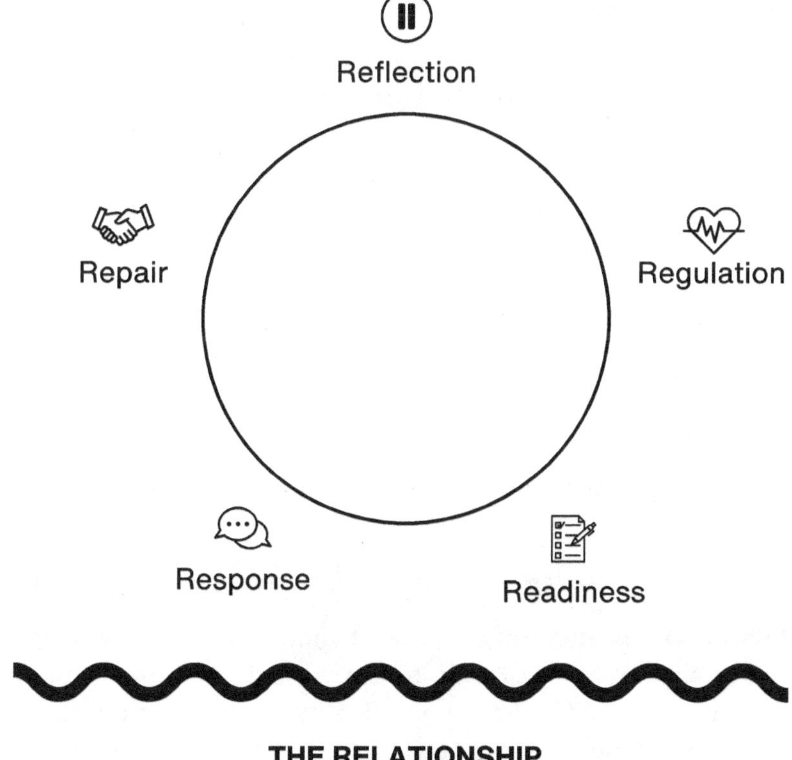

Figure 1: The Five R model of Smart Conflict
Source: Driscoll & van Haarst, 2023

The key mindset shift: Understanding Task Conflict vs Relational Conflict

The notion of Smart Conflict has been born out of a core, proven premise that not all conflict is equal. And as we advocate for you to lean into having *more* conflict at work rather than less, we mean the right kind of conflict. And a key element of Smart Conflict is that the conflict you do have is *task focused*.

Organizational psychologist Karen Jehn was the first to distinguish between two fundamentally different types of workplace conflict: Task Conflict and Relational Conflict.[1]

Task Conflict is characterized by disagreements and differing views on how the work itself should be done – the strategy, priorities or processes. Research shows that when teams engage in healthy debate over ideas and problems they are more effective, with enhanced critical thinking, improved decision-making and problem-solving leading to better outcomes.

Signs include:

- Focus on what is being done, not personal attributes.
- Intellectual engagement rather than emotional tension.
- Openness to hearing different viewpoints and refining ideas.
- Potential for creativity, provided it is managed constructively.

Relational Conflict, on the other hand, focuses on the people (rather than the ideas) and feels personal (because it is). It concentrates on differences in personality, values, communication styles, or relational dynamics and tensions (like power and control). Unlike Task Conflict, high Relational Conflict harms performance, creates emotional friction, erodes trust, and results in poor decision making as it has little to do with the best interests of the work itself.

Signs include:

- Feeling personally attacked or disrespected.
- Conflict centring around who is involved rather than what the issue is.
- Emotional responses like frustration, resentment or defensiveness.
- Difficulty resolving the issue because it's tied to identity or self-worth.

If we are being smart, we want to increase Task Conflict and minimize Relational Conflict at work to optimize for growth. The first step in Smart Conflict is to develop the ability to recognize which type of conflict you are involved in most often.

Figure 2: Relational vs Task Conflict
Source: Driscoll & van Haarst, 2025

Get into the sandpit

So what do we do if we notice we are in a Relational Conflict? How do we effectively move towards Task Conflict? Making the shift from Relational Conflict to Task Conflict requires you to reframe the conversation to depersonalize and redirect the focus to the shared goal.

Getting into the sandpit – or sandboxing, as it's more commonly known in design thinking and in the startup ecosystem – refers to a metaphorical space where you can test ideas, processes or prototypes free of the fear of failure. It's an environment that encourages experimentation, and is highly collaborative and exploratory in nature. It's the perfect place for Task Conflict to thrive – and we often ask clients who are in stalemate and heading into a Destructive Conflict to invite each other 'into the sandpit' to signal their intent to shift into Smart Conflict and generate solutions to get unstuck.

To activate the sandpit effectively we need to ensure our goal is focused on getting it right, not being right; practise showing up with an equal mix of confidence in our ability to find solutions but humility about our own ideas; and support everyone in the conversation to adopt an open, safe and curious headspace, perhaps by agreeing some rules of engagement (such as '*in this space there is no such thing as a bad idea*', '*we commit to saying "yes and", rather than "yes but"*'; and '*when we don't agree, we get curious, not furious*'). The beauty of this metaphorical sandpit is that at any point, if it's clear you're not building anything useful, any one of you can politely decide it's time to get out while still appreciating the contributions that took place. If it doesn't work the first time, it could be that you hadn't quite defined the right problem (or task) to solve. The important thing is to commit to returning again (perhaps next time with some different tools or new ideas), until you get it right.

The relationship is everything

You'll see under the Five R cycle in Figure 1 the wiggly line which represents the relationship between you and everyone in your working life you interact with. One of the most important ideas to hold on to as we take you through the methods of Smart Conflict is that it's the relationship that underpins *everything*. How successfully we are able to navigate hard conversations depends on the levels of trust, harmony and mutual respect that exist between you and the person on the other side of the table or the screen.

The technical term for this is *rapport* which the psychologist Kristin Neff defines as '*a sense of connection in which individuals feel psychologically aligned and understood by one another.*'[2] This might initially sound a bit overwhelming, but it shouldn't be – you don't have to be deeply connected with and aligned to everyone you meet to have successful relationships and good conversations. But it's important to realize that we are establishing a level of rapport with other people all the time through all our interactions – the friendly chat with your usual barista, the waved hello to the other parent on the school run, the shared in-joke with the IT helpdesk after your laptop suffers yet another dousing of spilled coffee.

Rapport is what creates goodwill between people and protects against moments of discord and disconnection. And the good news is that it's the work of moments: moments that build that goodwill and trust over time. It's created by signalling warmth and liking towards the other person through our words, actions, body language and tone of voice. Expressions of warmth and liking are shown in research to also be key to the development of friendship – we like people who we perceive like us.[3] When we naturally get on with someone and the relationship is going well, we tend to do this unconsciously and naturally, and the shared sense of rapport builds the strength and resilience of that relationship. But when we encounter people we don't gel with (or actively dislike), or we have a disagreement or experience tension with a colleague or friend we normally get on with, these signals of warmth and liking can quickly evaporate in the heat of a potential conflict, reducing rapport and causing damage to the relationship.

And this is where Smart Conflict comes in. We can consciously choose to build rapport with others to build good working relationships, even with those with whom we don't feel a natural connection, and even when we don't have a shared set of values or even understand where the other person is coming from. It's in our power to create the environment for effective conversations and Healthy Conflict, but we do have to do the work to make it happen. By working through the Five Rs we'll guide you through each element of how you can do this and give you the tools to start straight away.

Unconditional positive regard – a powerful tool for creating rapport

Before we leave the subject of rapport, we'd like to share with you a concept that was central to our coach training, and which is critical to our effectiveness as conflict coaches and educators – Unconditional Positive Regard. Carl Rogers – widely seen as one of the most influential psychologists of the 20th century – is best known for developing Person-Centred Therapy, which has become one of the major modalities used in counselling and psychotherapy today.[4] Rogers' fundamental belief was that people have the capacity for self-growth if they are provided with the right conditions. We can help to create these conditions for others by how *we* show up in the conversation. And you don't have to be a therapist to do it, anyone can.

Rogers believed that the three core conditions for personal growth are:

1) Unconditional Positive Regard – accepting people without judgement.
2) Empathy – understanding and reflecting their feelings.
3) Congruence (or Genuineness) – being authentic rather than distant or impersonal.

Hard conversations are essential for growth, as they are often where our greatest personal and professional learning takes place. But the conditions must be right for this growth to happen and for us (or the other person) not to simply ignore or reject what is being said.

One of the best ways to start creating these conditions is to practise getting into a mindset of Unconditional Positive Regard before you enter into a potentially hard conversation. The most important elements of this are to (a) suspend judgement of the other person, their ideas and their values, and, even if you don't agree with them, commit to listen and stay curious; and (b) assume positive intent – that in their own way they mean well and are doing their best, even if it's hard to understand how they are behaving.

Visit www.thepowerhouse/company/resources for a step-by-step guide to practising unconditional positive regard in hard conversations.

The outsized importance of repair

While each of the Five Rs is important in its own right, and to be adept at Smart Conflict it's important to understand how they work together, it might be tempting to skim this book for the 'how to' tips and tricks for hard conversations without reading cover to cover. We know this because we both buy more personal development and business books than we could realistically read in a lifetime, and often skim for the highlights ourselves. However, if there is one R we urge you not to skip, it's *Repair*.

Even if you have done lots of on the job 'soft skills' training (we dislike this term as interpersonal skills are absolutely critical to business outcomes – nothing soft about them) it's very unlikely any of the courses on feedback or communications will have covered the cycle of rupture and repair, which is present in all relationships, including those at work. It's essential to understand that all relationships that have any significance to us at all will have moments of rupture, where there's a break or damage of some sort. And it's not just the big blow ups that matter. The tiny moments of disconnection, misattunement or emotional unavailability count too.[5] It's impossible to have meaningful relationships without rupture, because none of us is perfect and human communication and emotions are so fraught with complexity. Although many of us feel we should try our best to avoid all conflict with our loved ones, friends and colleagues, this isn't what we should be striving for. Relationships free of rupture are also most likely free from depth and growth. But sometimes it's the smallest hurt or the seemingly throw-away comment that plants the seed that grows into a major conflict. That's why it's critical we learn to sense when a rupture has taken place and take action to repair it as soon as possible. We'll explain how to do this in the *Repair* chapter.

In their 50 years of research into adult relationships in their famous *Love Lab*, Drs. John and Julie Gottman – two of the world's preeminent relationship researchers – consistently found that relationship success is *not* about avoiding conflict – it's about repairing it effectively.

As Julie Gottman says:

> 'What distinguishes the masters of relationships from the disasters, is that when the masters mess up, they repair.'[6]

So, if you take nothing else away from the book, then remember this:

> Even if a hard conversation goes wrong, most conflicts can be repaired. It's what you do afterwards that matters.

Note to reader (otherwise known as: Health warning)

A word of caution

Before you move on to learning about the Five Rs in detail, a word of caution before you dive in. In the past we have seen clients (a couple of them in extremely senior positions) who are so inspired by these techniques they immediately go out and start challenging conversations with everyone in their path without fully understanding the Five R model… with mixed success, shall we say. Before you start, it is important to understand how the Five Rs work together, and to particularly appreciate the outsized importance of Repair when it comes to having hard conversations.

Staying safe in workplace conflict

It's also important that in using this book you think about staying safe as you navigate workplace conflict and hard conversations – psychologically, reputationally and physically. Depending on your specific circumstances, the particular situations you'd like to manage, and your own 'default settings' in terms of reactivity to stress there will be varying levels of risk in each of these categories. We urge you to check in with yourself and literally and/or metaphorically 'read the room' before you wade in, even if you have meticulously planned the conversation you want to have and are raring to go. The chapters on *Regulation* and *Readiness* will help with how to do this in practice.

In most modern workplaces it's our experience that the risk of physical harm from a conversation getting out of hand is very low indeed, and the penalties in such a circumstance would be extremely high. However, we have worked with clients in some settings where physical violence has been either threatened (but not carried out) or has actually taken place as a result of an escalation of an originally fairly minor disagreement.

Some industries and a small number of organizations within them will unfortunately bear the legacy of once tolerated but now unacceptable norms of behaviour, ranging from what we might call 'a culture of incivility' (i.e. being rude or verbally aggressive to colleagues, particularly juniors), to archaic practices such as resolving a dispute between two salespeople over a large client commission by having a planned and witnessed fistfight in the basement (true story). If you work somewhere where you feel you might have reason to fear the consequences of speaking up, please seek professional advice and support before trying to resolve the situation at hand (and consider looking for a new job in a setting where this isn't a factor you have to worry about).

Getting support

Even in the most professional and well-run organizations, there are times when a conflict at work – particularly a situation that has gone on for a while despite your best efforts – needs some additional support to resolve. There are times when cross words might cross a line. If you are uncomfortable or unhappy with a situation, or feel you don't have the skills or personal resources to handle it by yourself, we would always urge you to speak to someone about your concerns and get help to move forward.

This could be from your Human Resources department or your manager (or another senior manager, if your line manager is the person you are having difficulty with). If you aren't sure who to speak to, open up to a trusted colleague or friend who isn't directly involved and get their thoughts. Please don't suffer in silence. It's our hope that the exercises in this book will help you to gain a perspective on your own role in a workplace conflict, and that the techniques will give you a framework to experiment with doing things differently. However, sometimes it's not 'six of one and half a dozen of the other.' Sometimes it's not you, and it really is them. If in doubt, ask for the advice and support of others to get things sorted out.

If your organization is very small, you don't have a Human Resources department, or you feel you need impartial external advice but can't afford or can't access an employment lawyer, there are many country-specific resources available online and a number of organizations who will offer confidential helplines.

A note on case studies

Throughout this book we include case studies, quotes and examples we have encountered in our coaching practice. To protect confidentiality we have changed identifying details, and edited some quotations for brevity and clarity. However, all the case studies we offer are drawn from real situations that we hope will bring Smart Conflict to life.

2

Quick-start guide

This quick-start guide helps you jump straight to the parts of this book you need, right when you need them.

Promotions and career progression

- *I need to tell someone they're not getting promoted.* → **Readiness, Response, Repair**
- *I want to talk to my boss about my future.* → **Readiness, Response**

Performance conversations

- *I have to give someone feedback they won't want to hear.* → **A note on Feedback Conversations**
- *I need to challenge a colleague who is resistant to feedback.* → **Response**
- *I need an underperformer to recognize they are underperforming* → **Readiness, Response**

- *I need to tell a high performer they have a key development gap holding them back.* → **Readiness, Repair**
- *I need to give feedback to someone who is facing personal challenges.* → **Reflection, Readiness**
- *I need to give feedback to someone more senior than me.* → **Readiness, Response**
- *A junior team member is struggling, but I don't want to micromanage.* → **Readiness, Repair**

Pay and fees conversations

- *I want to ask for a pay rise.* → **Readiness**
- *I have to tell someone they won't get a pay rise.* → **Readiness, Response**
- *I need to negotiate fees with a client.* → **Readiness, Response**

Leadership and team performance

- *I have to set clear expectations for a high-stakes project.* → **Readiness, Response**
- *Tensions in my team are affecting performance.* → **Reflection, Response, Repair**

Co-founder challenges

- *We're not aligned on the company's direction.* → **Reflection, Readiness**
- *I've had a fall out with my co-founder – what now?* → **Repair**
- *I don't trust my co-founder* → **Reflection**

After the conflict: What now?

- *I was too harsh, and now I feel bad.* → **Repair**

- *I should have spoken up, but I didn't.* → **Response**
- *The other person blew up, and now things feel awkward.* → **Repair**
- *I need to apologize, but I also want to stand by my point.* → **Repair, Response**
- *We argued, but nothing really got resolved.* → **Repair, Readiness**
- *I think I might have upset them* → **Reflect, Repair**
- *I let someone walk all over me, and I need to reset.* → **Regulate, Response**

If you still disagree but need to move forward

- *We don't see eye to eye, but we have to work together.* →**Reflection, Readiness, Repair**
- *We both feel strongly, and I'm not sure how to find a middle ground.* → **Reflection, Readiness**

If trust is damaged

- *I feel like they don't trust me anymore.* → **Reflection**
- *I don't fully trust them after what happened.* → **Reflection**
- *The conflict exposed deeper issues in our relationship.* → **Reflection, Repair**

If you're feeling stuck

- *I don't know if I should bring it up or let it go.* → **Readiness**
- *I'm still mad, but I know I need to move on.* → **Regulate, Repair**

When you're caught off guard

- *I just got called into a difficult conversation and I have no time to prepare.* → **Regulate, Response**
- *Someone just gave me unexpected negative feedback, and I'm in a tailspin.* → **Regulate, Response**
- *A colleague just got emotional, and I don't know what to do or say.* → **Response, Repair**

When you need to hold your boundaries

- *A colleague or client is making unreasonable demands.* → **Readiness, Response**
- *A team member keeps overstepping their role.* → **Readiness, Response**

PART 1

UNDERSTANDING CONFLICT AT WORK

3

Why we fear conflict in life and work

The drive to prioritize our relationships

To understand our very human relationship with conflict we need to understand how our brains function, and the drives that evolved to protect us in our early cave-dwelling days from very real threats (like '*Am I going to eat it, or is it going to eat me?*'), drives which can still be activated in response to much more run-of-the-mill stresses today. Falling out with people did not, and does not, make us feel safe; it makes us feel extremely vulnerable. Humans are hardwired for connection, and want and need to feel they belong in groups.[1] A core part of the human experience is to care for others, and feel cared for, too. In prehistoric times, being rejected or abandoned by our community, losing the safety in numbers and the access to shared resources was a literal and immediate threat to our survival. Human connection is also critical to well-being and to the sense of having a life worth living. In her 2012 book *The Top Five Regrets of the Dying*, Bronnie Ware, a Palliative Care Nurse, documented that many people as they approach their later and final years emphasize that they wish they had invested more time connecting with friends and family, and had had the courage to express their true feelings more often.[2] To quote the renowned couples therapist Esther Perel, '*the quality of our relationships determines the quality of our lives*'.

So it follows that often our instincts will be to protect our relationships above all else. In the modern world this powerful drive can extend to protecting our sense of belonging to our work 'tribes': the teams and organizations we work for, even the clients we serve. It can drive how we think about the meanings of our job titles, how we feel about our position in a hierarchy, how we contribute to collective work performance and results, and how willing we are to speak up against other members of the group and potentially risk those relationships. It can lead us to seek harmony, even if this is artificial.

None of this is a bad thing in itself. We want you to continue to make social connections and quality relationships a top priority, because the impact of this on the quality of your life couldn't be more enormous; in fact it's a matter of life and death. A 2015 study by Julianne Holt-Lunstad et al. from Brigham Young University[3] looked at every aspect of people's lifestyles including their diet, exercise, marital status, whether they smoked and how much they drank, then followed up seven years later to see who was still living. She concluded that close connections with others and good social integration (how much you interact with others as you move through your day, even with those you don't know well) were the biggest predictors of reduced risk of mortality, even more so than diet, exercise or smoking. And having good quality relationships with your workmates – people you might spend more time with than anyone in your life – is likely to have a major positive impact on your well-being.

And what about hybrid working? Some further research by the neuroscientist Elizabeth Redcay et al. in 2010 suggests that in-person connection has more of a positive impact on our brain function than virtual connections (she hypothesizes this might be a key determining factor in why women typically outlive men as they prioritize in-person interaction), but if that's not always possible any connection – including by phone or video call – is still good connection.[4]

Conflict = damaged relationships?

So, yes, our instinct to protect and prioritize our relationships and social connections is essential and to be encouraged. But when it comes to hard conversations many of us are making two fundamentally flawed assumptions. The first is the assumption that *any* kind of hard conversation will be damaging to the relationship. In fact what we know to be true is exactly the opposite. A 2002 study by Tjosvold and Sun found that relationships with a total absence of conflict are weaker than those where conflicted moments and conversations happen.[5] But we need the right kind of conflict, the healthy Smart Conflict that builds and strengthens our relationships. Like the Japanese art of Kintsugi, where broken objects are repaired with liquid gold (a much more precious repair tool than superglue), precisely because it highlights the cracks and events of the past, creating something arguably even more beautiful in its repaired state than in its pure original form. For people, we too can think of our disagreements and fallings-out as an opportunity to re-bond with some relational liquid gold, but only if we take the time to intentionally and competently make the repair (see the chapter on *Repair* for more on how to do this well).

So the first reason we fear hard conversations is because we falsely believe that any conflict is damaging, when in fact this is only true of destructive, relational conflict. All the evidence points to Smart Conflict actively strengthening our bonds.

Clear is kind

The second big assumption many make is that the kindest thing to do is to *not* tell someone a hard truth for fear of upsetting them. When we are hardwired to prioritize connection, being honest can feel deeply uncomfortable, with feelings of rejection even manifesting as physical pain[6] and mental anxiety, especially if we are not practised at giving or receiving honest feedback. This fear of rejection, judgement and ruptured relationships creates and reinforces what we might think of as an 'honesty gap' – the difference between what we say vs what we are really thinking.

We would challenge the kindness of depriving someone of the opportunity for personal and professional growth, which is what sits on the other side of developmental feedback if we do it well. Without insight from others on the impact we are having, it's not possible to know if our intentions are landing as we mean them to. And often they are falling short. When we hold back from sharing information that is critical to enabling people to reach their goals, we keep them in what psychologist Nevitt Sanford termed the Comfort Zone,[7] which paradoxically is not very comfortable at all. The thing about the comfort zone is that although we feel highly supported, we are not being stretched in any way. In their seminal book *Intrinsic Motivation and Self-Determination in Human Behavior*, Edward Deci and Richard Ryan outline the human innate desire for growth and progress.[8] By withholding hard truths, we are complicit in keeping people stagnating at their current competency level, rather than helping them reach their full potential. In our masterclasses we introduce the idea that 'clear is kind,' and explore the idea that saying what we really think – with kindness, and bolstered by support – creates clarity and certainty, which in turn builds trust, confidence and the motivation to take action to improve (even when what we are hearing is hard to hear).

Anger – the forbidden feeling

Another reason we fear conflict is because for many of us, anger has been demonized as the 'unacceptable' or 'inappropriate' emotion. And it's understandable, because anger is a powerful feeling that can lead to some pretty unsavoury and threatening behaviours. Being in the presence of anger, or simply sensing it rising in ourselves, can feel pretty dangerous. The problem is not feeling angry. The problem is the way people sometimes *behave* when they feel angry. And in our experience, most people who struggle with unacceptable or antisocial angry outbursts do not feel in control of their behaviour in the moment. The behaviour often doesn't feel like a choice, but an irresistible force.

Shaming ourselves or others for these reactions is not conducive to supporting anyone to stop losing their temper at work. They are likely feeling ashamed enough already. Instead, we should support increasing their self-awareness that the behaviour is holding them back, and damaging both their relationships and probably their reputation at work.

It's no wonder we are cautious – or even afraid – of anger at work. Unexpected outbursts of strong emotion or displays of aggression can feel very frightening indeed. The automatic threat responses (fight, flight and freeze) we've inherited from our prehistoric ancestors can have a powerful effect on our nervous system, giving us a sense of psychological or physical danger irrespective of whether we are the originator, in the vicinity, or on the receiving end of it.

We get it, it feels unpleasant. And the consequences of acting on it can be regrettable. But feeling angry is a fundamental part of being human, it's unavoidable, and we all experience it sometimes. It's not going anywhere. And we don't actually want it to. It's a fundamental part of the human stress responses that have evolved to keep us safe. There are occasions – particularly when we are under the kind of threat that involves real danger – where anger and aggression can be actively protective, even life saving. The move to shame all anger, particularly in the workplace, is not helping people lean into the hard but critical conversations. Such is their fear of being judged for having strong negative feelings, many suppress or choose to hide them altogether.

Is it harder than ever to disagree at work?

This is a question we are often asked, and one that's difficult to answer in any concrete terms. But it is likely that our confidence and ability to have difficult conversations is directly correlated to the complexity levels of our workplaces at any given time. Most people would agree that navigating organizational culture – the rules and boundaries for 'how we get things done around here' – in modern workplaces has never been more complex, contributing to increasing anxiety and fear around speaking up confidently. When we are trying to understand our leadership and conflict-coaching clients' behaviour, and the themes and patterns of behaviours within the workforces of client organizations we support, we always consider the wider systemic factors that are in play.

Global political narratives

In considering this question we look first to those key societal shifts that are being felt around the world. Awareness of deeply complex geopolitical conflicts and humanitarian struggles is higher than ever with the advent of 24-hour rolling news, and the ubiquity of social media feeding a never-ending stream of new information. However in recent decades there has been a move towards ever more polarized political narratives driving fear, division and intolerance, which can impact how we show up in our own teams and groups, both in and out of work. Echo chambers driven by online platforms and mainstream media can provoke a sense of threat from 'others', whoever they may be. We become more anxious, resorting to the perceived safety of more exclusive, 'tribal' behaviours in our own lives and communities as we desperately seek a sense of order and security.

Cancel culture

The normalization of online trolling – the deliberate act of provoking, harassing or upsetting others on the internet by posting inflammatory, off-topic or disruptive messages – is another systemic reality that is instilling fear in many of our clients to share a point of view on anything (both on and offline). Many people harbour a fear that if they speak up, they risk being misunderstood, having their words twisted and ultimately being shamed and 'cancelled'. We've heard from many senior leaders in our masterclasses and workshops that they feel confused and exhausted by what they are experiencing as fast-moving and evolving social rules and regulations as to what is ok to say and how they can say it without causing offence (both in and out of work). Whether you believe in the existence of cancel culture or not, it's clear in our work that a perception of it as a real possibility is driving avoidant behaviour in some organizations.

In our experience it's not just the older generations who are finding the working landscape hard to navigate. Those in their early careers today are often arriving with very different ideas about what work means to those their managers may have developed as juniors a decade before. Many of our leadership clients report that their younger staff are much more aware of work-life balance, and of mental health and well-being, and are more willing to create and hold boundaries around working hours and conditions. While this has to be a good thing – overwork and burnout is something we see far too much in our practice – it also creates a landscape where there can be very different expectations about what 'having a work ethic' and a high performance culture means.

What the teams we work with have reported to us is that, as a side effect, they are less inclined to lean in to any kind of difficult conversation, including giving performance feedback or telling employees when they've done something wrong. As one leader in a consulting firm told us: '*I honestly just don't even give feedback anymore to the team. It's too complicated, and I have no clue how to do it without getting into hot water. I could do without it.*'

Virtual working

When it comes to hard conversations, virtual working presents some new challenges, which if not carefully tackled head on can lead to having fewer conversations that matter. There are several elements that set teams up to fail here, the first of which is the simple fact that if we have only ever met our colleagues remotely, it's going to require more concerted effort to develop a depth of connection than for those people we have spent face to face time with. This matters because the strength of our connection is directly correlated with our ability to effectively manage and overcome challenges together.

In almost all contexts, having a hard conversation, even a smart one, is usually the last thing we feel like doing. But when we are working remotely, without the opportunity for serendipitous meetings, we have to consciously decide to request a meeting in order to start the conversation. With no watercooler moments to provide opportunities for those 'ah, while I've got you...' conversations, it's all too easy for us to not have the conversation at all, or convince ourselves we'll do it tomorrow. But we don't.

The era of 'the empathetic leader'

In our work as team coaches we work with leadership teams to support them to move towards their highest collective performance. One of the most common challenges they bring to the work we do together is the tension they experience around holding others to account regarding their responsibilities, in an era of leadership that (for good reason) emphasizes understanding and empathy as key leadership qualities. But we may have collectively thrown the baby out with the bath water.

Many of the leaders and managers we meet have made the assumption that they must make a choice between being an empathetic leader or a results driven one. They are utterly confused about how to integrate both, and feel stuck between seemingly competing demands – the human one, and the business one. But empathy and accountability are not mutually exclusive. In fact they can and *must* co-exist for high performance because both are core factors of effectively motivating others. We can empathize by showing our confidence in the person and offering our support to solve the problem, whilst simultaneously holding firm on the goal and results we want to achieve. In his 2013 book *Boundaries for Leaders: Results, Relationships, and Being Ridiculously in Charge*, Dr. Henry Cloud summarizes this with '*go hard on the issue, soft on the person.*'[9] Making it clear that the issue needs to be resolved whilst offering to collaborate on finding solutions, while also communicating '*I believe you can get there*' ensures we motivate without blame, shame or judgement. Approaching it with compassion and clarity means we are much more likely to get the performance we need from our colleagues and teams.

Whilst the systemic factors we've outlined so far are not within our control to change, building your awareness of them does enable you to have more compassion for why any of us might struggle with hard conversations and provides us with the opportunity to make more conscious and considered decisions about leaning into them *despite* the systemic challenges. Challenges which are unlikely to go away anytime soon, and are better navigated than ignored.

Not knowing how to do it

There is one final reason we might fear conflict at work, one that *is* totally within your control to change – and that is, not feeling equipped to do it successfully.

When we know something is important but we don't know how to do it, it's only natural we feel hesitant and fearful, and swerve doing it wherever possible. For most of us this is not just a case of imposter syndrome or self-doubt, we probably haven't been taught how to have Smart Conflict, so we could say our concerns that we might not get it right are totally valid. What we have seen in our work time and time again is that deciding to invest your time and energy in upskilling in Smart Conflict will pay dividends for you, your team and your organization.

Find your 'why'

To close out this chapter, reflecting on the challenges we've outlined, we encourage you to reflect on your personal 'why' for having hard conversations and to think about this at an identity level. Completing the following statements might help you do this:

> *It's important for me to have hard conversations at work because…*
>
> *I have hard conversations at work because I believe…*
>
> *I'm the sort of person who has hard conversations because a core value of mine is…*

If you're struggling to find your why, we'd recommend heading back to the *Introduction* for some very persuasive data on the transformational upside of leaning into hard conversations at work (and every area of your life).

4
The influence of genetics, family, culture and gender

'We are like chameleons, we take our hue and the color of our moral character from those who are around us.'[1] – John Locke

In this chapter, we'll look at the influences that inform our adult default conflict styles and responses, exploring why we are the way we are. As with many things, the roots of our approach to conflict were formed in our early family life and the dynamics we experienced there as children, so that's where we'll start our exploration.

Our personal history

As adults, our behaviours often mirror the way we saw our very first caregivers role-model for us. John Bowlby's attachment theory[2] (and later Mary Ainsworth's research on attachment styles)[3] suggests that these early interactions set out our norms and scripts for how we go on to think about and manage conflicts in later life.

John, a manager in a media agency, grew up in a household where surface-level disagreements were rare to non-existent and conflict was avoided at all costs, but passive-aggressive silences were very much the norm. John was referred to us for 1:1 coaching by his head of department because as an adult he had become a professional conflict avoider, prioritizing maintaining harmony over any risk of rocking the boat by pushing his low-performing team to raise their game. This head-in-sand approach was holding John back from achieving the promotion he so desperately wanted. And this wasn't the only problem. Over the course of our work with John, it became clear that in prioritizing the needs of others, John had spent years neglecting his own. He had no idea how to start asking for what he wanted. John had compromised himself and held back the team's growth by following a script he had learned in childhood. One that had gone unchallenged until this point.

Amrita, a Chief Technology Officer in a biotech firm, had a very different personal history. Amrita grew up in a household with a large extended family, where the smallest squabble seemed to turn into a full-blown showdown. Doors were slammed, voices were raised, dramatic exits were made. It *was* loud and dramatic, but Amrita maintained she always felt safe, and admitted she found some satisfaction in giving as good as she got. This experience led to Amrita reflecting that her norms around conflict were often at odds with her colleagues', who seemed to her in the main to be overly sensitive. What for Amrita felt like a run-of-the-mill, entirely tolerable disagreement, could be experienced by others as an aggressive row. This had led her to being labelled as emotional, confrontational and 'difficult' and heading towards being put on a performance improvement plan, before deciding she needed to do some serious work on her conflict style.

For Tosin, an academic researcher who grew up in France, lively debate was a normal part of family life around the dinner table. But sometimes debates could take a turn that left Tosin feeling overwhelmed, confused and scared. When provoked, his father had a temper that resulted in what Tosin recalls as '*a lot of shouting, and me feeling generally pretty afraid of him*'. Today Tosin's instinct is to avoid conflict situations wherever possible, suppressing his feelings and in his words 'implode' (collapse internally under the weight of his emotions) rather than allowing them to explode.

Even in homes without high-running emotions, a child raised by strict, authoritarian parents, for instance, may as an adult default to seeking to assert control and demand compliance from others in moments of disagreement. For children whose caregivers demonstrated empathy and active listening at tense moments, it will most likely be easier to reenact these same conflict resolution strategies in adulthood. Our responses to our early childhood experiences are unique to us, and we can't and won't fit into neat boxes, but our childhood experiences of conflict can provide clues to understanding how we feel about and behave in hard conversations today. In the *Reflection* chapter we'll take you through some exercises to explore how your personal history might have shaped how you show up.

The influence of siblings

We can't talk about our childhood experiences without mentioning the role of siblings. For many of us they are our original sparring partners, giving us a crash course in conflict management. It's likely that alongside them we honed our negotiation skills, learning about power dynamics, the art of compromise (or getting your own way), how to use humour to diffuse tense situations, or how to say sorry and move on from a particularly nasty spat.

Research published in 2022 by Professor Gentrit Berisha and his colleagues[4] indicates that your position in the sibling hierarchy can influence your conflict resolution style. Their study, involving 230 managers from a variety of industries, found that birth order may play a role in shaping conflict-handling, with firstborns preferring problem-solving approaches, middle children leaning towards compromising and peacekeeping strategies, while the youngest children use both compromising and problem-solving methods in conflicts. Those with no siblings were found to be more likely to be avoidant when it comes to conflict, perhaps having less opportunity in their early years to test and learn how to handle it through the daily tussles and frustrations of sibling life.

Looking forward

Whatever our personal histories, it's worth remembering that our past does not have to define our future. Whilst our childhood experiences lay the groundwork for our default conflict styles, they are not necessarily hardwired and immutable. Neuroscience research has shown that through the incredible process of neuroplasticity we possess the ability to rewire our brains, to modify and transform our approach and behaviours, including how we manage and respond to conflict (see Norman Doidge's seminal books *The Brain That Changes Itself* and *The Brain's Way of Healing* to find out more about how neuroplasticity works).[5] Is it easy? No, but we have an opportunity to 'choose our hard'. We can do the difficult work of getting better at hard conversations now, for an easier life later, or choose to avoid the short-term effort and pain of changing, and deal with a lifetime of Destructive Conflict. We know which one we would choose. And if you're reading this book, you've already taken the first step on your journey to change.

The role of genetics

While the science is highly complex, and fascinating new evidence on genetics and epigenetics (how our environment affects the expression of our genes – simplistically, whether they are turned 'on' or 'off') is emerging every day, we know from research that genetic factors can influence personality traits such as aggression, anxiety and emotional regulation, which all play a role in how someone handles conflict.[6] Empathy, crucial for conflict resolution, may also be influenced by genetics, with some people predisposed to higher levels of empathy.[7] Genetic factors may even play a role in shaping conflict styles – there is research that suggests that some individuals may naturally avoid conflict, while others are more confrontational.[8]

Neurodiversity can also have a significant influence on how individuals experience, interpret and respond to relational conflict, often in nuanced ways. Neurodiversity refers to the natural range of variation in human brain function and behavioural traits and generally recognizes conditions such as those on the autism spectrum, attention deficit hyperactivity disorder (ADHD), dyslexia and dyspraxia (also referred to as Developmental Coordination Disorder). While it's estimated that around 15 to 20% of the population globally are neurodivergent,[9] variations in access to diagnosis and an evolving understanding of how conditions may affect individuals more subtly may mean that this figure is an underestimate. Research on neurodiversity at work is still a relatively new field and each person's experience is highly personal, so generalizations can be unhelpful.

However, it's important to be aware of how neurodiversity may influence how people can have a very different experience of the same conversation. For example, individuals with autism spectrum condition or other neurodivergent profiles may process social cues – like tone of voice, facial expressions or implied meaning – differently from neurotypical peers,[10] and misinterpretation of intent or emotion on both sides can escalate or prolong a conflict. Conditions like ADHD, dyslexia and dyspraxia may involve challenges with emotional regulation, speed of language processing or heightened sensitivity to stimuli, leading some individuals to being more prone to overwhelm or withdrawal in high-stress or emotionally charged situations.[11] While we are not specialists in neurodiversity, many of the techniques we suggest in this book will help to create conversational environments that invite diverse perspectives, foster awareness of how another person is experiencing a hard conversation, allow space for everyone to regulate themselves according to their needs, and structure clear but kind communication and get back on track when things take an unexpected turn.

Understanding culture codes

The cultures we were raised in, or have spent time immersed in, will have also shaped our conflict behaviours and norms. In her book *The Culture Map*, Erin Meyer explores how cultural differences shape communication, leadership and collaboration in global business and provides a framework for understanding workplace behaviours across cultures.[12] This includes a fascinating scale that identifies how much communication relies on sub-text in different cultures: what she has called High Context vs Low Context Cultures.

Meyer defines High Context Cultures as those which rely heavily on implicit, nuanced communication and non-verbal cues. Direct communication is actively discouraged, and it is expected that a listener will 'read between the lines' to get the message. She identifies Japan, China, India, Brazil, Mexico and many Middle Eastern countries as High Context cultures. When it comes to conflict, open confrontation is often seen as rude and disrespectful, so disagreements are typically handled privately and in a more indirect way.

Low Context Cultures are defined by their reliance on explicit, direct and clear communication, with a focus on the spoken word, and far less on non-verbal cues. The US, Germany, The Netherlands, the UK and Australia are identified by Meyer as Low Context Cultures. These cultures are much more comfortable with direct and open confrontation, which is seen as playing a critical role in effective problem solving, and the giving of feedback is encouraged.

Meyer also offers a second relevant and useful set of categorizations for understanding cultural differences when it comes to conflict and hard conversations: Collectivist vs Individualistic Cultural Codes. In Collectivist cultures (including Japan, China and Mexico) group harmony and cohesion are prioritized, so conflict is approached cautiously and consensus-building is prioritized for decision making. Feedback is given indirectly and communicated more often than not through non-verbal cues (tone of voice, facial expressions, use of silence or pauses, gestures or body language) or even through third parties in an effort to maintain group harmony. And, just like those High Context nations, Collectivist cultures will go out of their way to avoid direct confrontation and manage disagreements discreetly.

By contrast, Individualistic Cultures (including the US, The Netherlands and Germany) prioritize assertiveness and self-expression, valuing individual autonomy over conformity, resulting in decisions more typically being made by dominant individuals. And much like Low Context cultures, value honest, direct and explicit feedback and tend to see open disagreement as a sign of healthy and constructive debate, leading to effective problem solving.

Although there is an obvious correlation between individualistic and low-context cultures, these styles all operate on a spectrum, and are not as binary as they might seem. There are also exceptions. For example, Sweden and Denmark are classed as Individualistic but sit more towards the High Context end of the spectrum, and France, whilst more Individualistic than many, is not categorized as a Low Context nation as sub-text (i.e. the implied but unsaid) forms a key part of its cultural communication style. It's reasonable to say that when it comes to hard conversations these varying expectations and norms can be a potential minefield – ripe for confusion and misunderstanding and often one of the major factors in a workplace conflict.

We were once called in to work on a Board coaching assignment with the international Board of a healthtech business. The Chair outlined to us the ongoing challenges they were facing in having constructive debate in board meetings, and his frustration and confusion about how some board members were behaving, which he found unprofessional and unhelpful. Stony silences, eye-rolling, nervous laughter and mixed signals on decisions were commonplace, and relations were becoming strained. Between them, Board members originated from Belgium, the UK, Germany, Italy, Brazil and Poland.

Where participants from the UK and Brazil reported finding meetings high conflict and stressful, with aggressive and otherwise boundary-crossing behaviour from others during disagreements, the German and Belgian participants reported how measured and effective discussions were. While the British CEO called the Board 'dysfunctional and combative', the very experienced Belgian Chair described it as 'one of the most harmonious Boards I've been part of'. The exact same meetings, with two totally opposing experiences. Our starting point for working with the Board as a group was to support them to better understand each other's cultural norms and expectations of each other, by helping them to more overtly signpost their intentions, to recognize when they had crossed a line and a repair needed to be made, and to agree a conflict code for how they would behave together moving forward, providing a shared language to hold each other to account on.

It's evident that misunderstandings can easily arise when cultural differences are in play: how easily a direct communicator could seem rude, or an indirect one evasive, when they share a different cultural context. Having an awareness that these cultural codes exist, and how different they can be, is an important starting point for any international teams who need to collaborate together.

The power of organizational culture

The norms that live explicitly or implicitly within your organizational culture will also directly influence how you handle difficult conversations at work. Many of us spend more time with our colleagues than our friends and family, so it's perhaps no surprise that our colleagues' behaviour would have an impact on our own behaviour. Such is our hardwired need to belong in groups (our ancient brain being back on that savanna, worried that alone we'll be taken by a cheetah), adopting dominant behaviours is an unconscious survival strategy that does a great job in ensuring we are more likely to be accepted as we avoid challenging the social norms.

This applies to all our behaviours, and explains, for example, why, despite being on time for meetings your entire career, on joining a new team where the norm is to start all meetings 10 minutes late as people trickle in slowly after the start time (no one seems to know why or when it started, but '*it's just the way we do things around here*'), we are very likely to find ourselves six months in also rocking up late, such is the pull to fit in and observe the social code (and maybe we got bored of sitting by ourselves for 10 minutes while everyone else got coffee).

Caroline, a Chief People Officer in a construction firm and 1:1 Coaching client had recently been headhunted into her dream job. The business was scaling fast but things were beginning to crumble around the edges. It was a classic case of what got us here almost certainly won't get us where we need to go next. The firm had gone out of their way to hire someone extremely experienced with a track record of transformational change. They were totally committed to succeeding with the next stage of business growth, and Caroline was a critical hire to enable it.

Caroline had been in post for nine months when we first met and she was feeling frustrated. Despite being brought in to deliver transformation, requiring her to challenge the status quo, she was met with deep resistance to any action she tried to take in real terms. Normally upbeat, enthusiastic and measured, she was finding herself increasingly short tempered and snappy, on occasion being seized with white-hot rage as she received another flat out 'no' to her meticulous proposals. Sadly, it's all too common for a CEO or Board to commit to an end goal, but not be willing to go on the journey to reach it. As the deeply uncomfortable, messy reality of what change involved emerged, and as the sacrifices needed became all too clear, they hit the brakes. The organization wouldn't just have to do things differently, it would have to *be* different. It would involve addressing behaviours and making decisions that would disrupt the organization's sense of identity and value system. Or in other words, its culture. With coaching, Caroline was able to take a step back from her frustration, stop being drawn into the aggressive tone being set, and resist getting swept away (and out of a job) with the tide of resistance she faced. Leaning into curiosity about the *lived* values she was witnessing – way out of step with the written values she'd had hand-painted on the fancy new office walls – allowed her to become fascinated by the culture-change task in front of her, and galvanized her to stay and do the hard work, one step at a time. As we write, she's still there, and seen as a critical catalyst of the company's growth. The culture's not perfect (yet) but it's getting there.

Differing gender expectations

So far, we've looked at how our personal histories and the cultures we've spent time in – societal and organizational – influence our individual conflict style and response. These influences are thought to be universal and not gender specific. But there are absolutely gender-specific cultural expectations for what is deemed acceptable and unacceptable in how women show up in difficult conversations and conflict moments compared to men. In fact the research shows that gender plays a significant role in how men and women experience, interpret and respond to hard conversations and conflict, often as a result of expected societal norms.[13]

In their 2018 book *How Women Rise*, Marshall Goldsmith and Sally Helgesen discuss the *double bind* that many women face in the workplace.[14] The double bind refers to the contradictory expectations placed on women in professional settings – specifically, that they need to be both warm and competent, but when they display confidence or assertiveness (traits often associated with leadership), they risk being perceived as less likeable or too aggressive. This creates a dilemma where if a woman is warm, collaborative and agreeable, she may be liked but not taken seriously. If she is assertive, direct and ambitious, she may be seen as competent but unlikeable or too 'pushy.' This paradox can make it difficult for women to advance in leadership roles, as they are often judged more harshly than men for the same behaviours. And by both men and women alike: Role Congruity Theory, developed by social psychologists Alice Eagly and Steven Karau reveals we all hold deep-seated biases in how leadership is perceived, regardless of our own sex. The broader evidence base supports this (see also the 2023 publication *Fix the System, Not the Women* by Laura Bates) and is certainly reflected in our consulting rooms in the challenges our female clients face in having their voices heard.

While fixing the system is a big (and whilst absolutely worthwhile, possibly endless) fight, our Smart Conflict approach aims to offer an alternative mindset to 'nice' when it comes to conflict, giving women confidence to speak up where worrying about being perceived unlikeable or aggressive is currently a constraint. And whilst we don't advocate for solutions that aim to 'fix the women, not the problem' we do want to highlight that research has shown that compared to men, women often adopt an avoidant conflict style, prioritizing peace making and relational harmony over Task Conflict[15] (see the *Regulation* chapter on the *tend and befriend* response to stress). And beyond fitting into societal norms, it seems women actually experience more anxiety and discomfort from conflict than men, resulting in a lower tolerance for disagreement, which can result in emotional burnout from the long-term deployment of conflict avoidance.[16]

In essence, Smart Conflict offers a way to disagree constructively that does not require women to be 'fixed', to ignore systemic biases or to make the choice between being either agreeable or aggressive. There's another, smarter way.

PART 2
THE SMART CONFLICT FIVE R MODEL

Introducing the Five R model

For the next five chapters we're going to take a deep dive into the Five R model of Smart Conflict. We see the Five Rs not as a to-do list to tick off, but as a cycle through which we can continually move as we hone our skills and are presented with new challenges. At times you may need to move back and forth between them, or focus more deeply on one than the others and allow that to be your focus for a while. For example, during periods of high stress you may need to double down on your regulation skills, to respond, not react. If you find someone really getting under your skin, you may need to reflect intensely on what it is that's causing your annoyance. During times of rapid change, your focus might be on ensuring your readiness to handle new situations, and scenario planning so that your response to the unexpected hits exactly the right tone. There will almost certainly be times when you realize that you need to take concerted action to repair a damaged relationship and restore goodwill… before reflecting on what you can learn from that experience to try and lessen the chances of it happening again.

You might also go back and forth between the Five Rs in the course of a single conversation – going in with your readymade Plan A, pausing to regulate when you find yourself thrown off course, giving yourself time to formulate a considered response to an objection, before going back to Plan A again for another try.

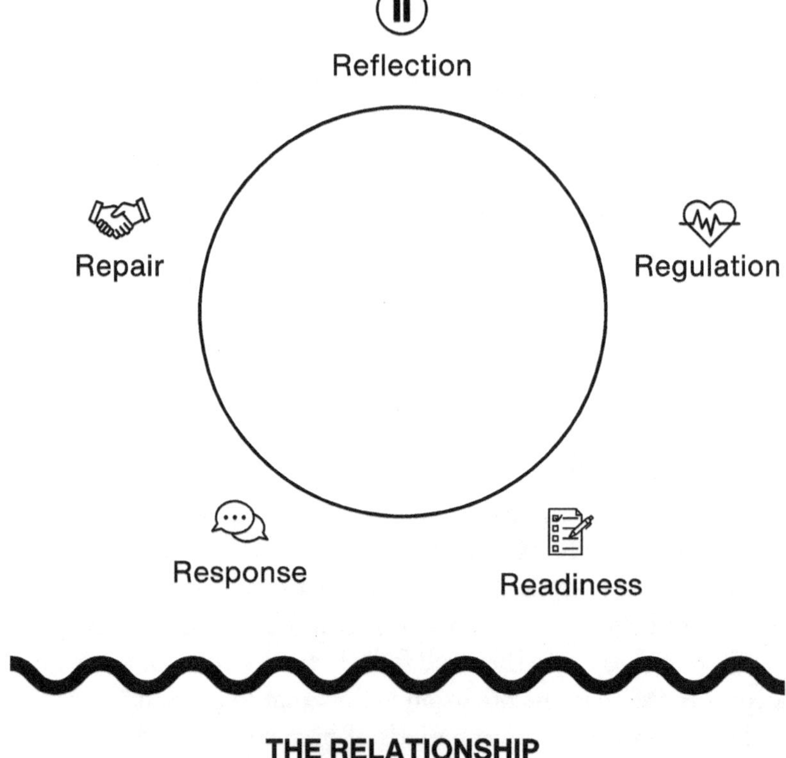

Figure 3: The Five R model of Smart Conflict revisited
Source: Driscoll & van Haarst, 2023

Your starting point for triaging each hard conversation will depend on what's needed in each situation: you can head back to the *Quick Start* guide if you need some immediate help.

However, in this book we will begin with *Reflection*, as deepening our understanding of ourselves and others is often a very good place to start.

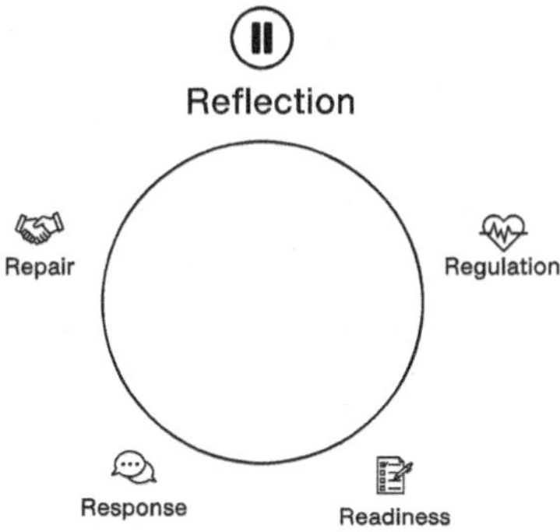

5 Reflection

'Until you make the unconscious conscious, it will direct your life and you will call it fate.' – Carl Jung[1]

Do you ever wonder why you react the way you do in difficult conversations and conflict? Why you keep quiet in meetings when inside you deeply disagree with what's being said? Why you feel personally attacked when someone disagrees with your ideas? Or why you feel the need to win an argument even when it's not the most important thing?

If you're curious about the answers to these kinds of questions, you're in the right place. In this chapter we'll share some of our favourite self-reflection tools to help you gain new insights as to why you are the way you are, and why you behave the way you do when it comes to hard conversations. Self-reflection is an act of accountability. By stepping back and thinking about how we show up today, we begin to paint a clearer picture of how that is influencing the situations we find ourselves in, and the people we find ourselves with. The more reflection we do, the more we increase our self-awareness – *'our conscious knowledge of one's own character, feelings, motives, and desires'*.[2] And the greater our self-awareness, the greater our ability to change our behaviours.

Taking the time to think about why we behave and respond in the way we do, and how we came to be who we are today, can sometimes provide such profound 'aha' moments that we are immediately able to break away from old patterns and default behaviours by simply deciding to let go of unhelpful approaches we've unconsciously committed to. This idea is known as 'making the link, to break the link' (a key component of psychodynamic and attachment-based therapeutic principles).

Unfortunately, for most of us it's not as simple as all that, and making the link is not enough alone to break us out of deeply ingrained behaviour patterns. Nonetheless, reflecting on how we, and those around us, show up in conflict (and why) is a useful exercise and a good place to start because it helps us identify what our default behavioural modes are, giving us insight into how our approach may no longer be working for us.

From here we can focus our energies on adapting and changing those behaviours that will make the biggest difference to our own, and our team's performance. Understanding the path we've walked that has led us to who we are today can also give us permission for more self-compassion and reduce personal shame for any unwanted and limiting behaviours, and perhaps even start to give us some clues as to why we always seem to end up in a confrontation with certain people and not others. With reflection we can both start our change journey, and refine it, transforming our experience of conflict for good. In the *Regulation*, *Readiness*, *Response* and *Repair* chapters we'll share with you the new behaviours you can choose and smart strategies you can use to change how you show up in a potential conflict at work.

Increasing your conflict self-awareness

We are introducing the following models, tools and exercises to support you to reflect on your personal relationship with conflict and increase your self-awareness when it comes to your default settings around conflict today. All the exercises in this chapter feature in our *Smart Conflict Workbook* available for download here: www.thepowerhouse.company/resources

Understand your family foundations

This first exercise asks you to think about the early origins of your default conflict style. By identifying the strategies you learned growing up, you will be better placed to consider how smartly they are working for you in the contexts you find yourself in today. It is inspired by and adapted from the work of renowned couples therapist Esther Perel.

This exercise should take about 10 minutes to complete. You might choose to sit somewhere quiet, or perhaps go for a walk with someone and talk through the questions one by one together. Take enough time to reflect on what's true for you, but try not to overthink them – don't worry about capturing your history perfectly. Often our instinctive response provides the most useful clues.

Reflective Questions:

1) How did people in your family disagree?
2) How was anger expressed? (Shouting? Sulking? Silent treatment? Sarcasm? Door slamming? Storming off? Crying?)
3) Who was (and was not) allowed to get angry?
4) Was conflict acknowledged or ignored?
5) After a conflict, how were things reconciled and resolved? Were they?

Introducing the six default conflict styles

Shaped by your origin story and other conditioning influences including cultural and environmental factors, your Default Conflict Style (or Styles) describes your automatic, habitual responses to a real or perceived conflict. They remain our autopilot 'go to' responses unless we consciously intervene to change them.

We developed our Default Conflict Style Model based on our own practice and experience as conflict coaches, and by synthesizing and building on the available evidence and theory, including the Thomas-Kilmann Conflict Mode Instrument (TKI), which is probably most widely known.[3]

Our Default Conflict Style Model can be used both to increase your own self-awareness of your default conflict styles(s), and as a diagnostic to consider how your colleagues or clients are showing up in hard conversations with you. As this chapter is focused on increasing our own self-awareness, we suggest starting there.

The model is built on two axes:

1) The vertical axis: your conflict confidence – related to the level of anxiety you experience when you think about having a hard conversation.

   High conflict confidence – you are unfazed by the idea of having a tense or confrontational conversation with someone. You think it's more important to have the conversation than to worry about how you or they might feel about it.

   Medium conflict confidence – you experience some anxiety and reluctance to have a conversation that could be unwelcome or become tense, but are willing to engage because you know it matters, and you're reasonably confident you're equipped to navigate it well (at least as well as anyone might be). You might still prepare carefully in advance what you're going to say and give yourself a pep talk to muster the courage to do it.

   Low conflict confidence – you feel overwhelmed at the very thought of confrontation and avoid it if at all possible. It's hard to imagine the conversation going well and it feels too hard to start it voluntarily. You don't believe that you or the other person has the resilience to cope with a conflict.

2) The horizontal axis: your desire to win – refers to your mindset going into a hard conversation – are you focused on being right, or getting it right?

   High desire to win – you argue forcefully, aiming to prove your point at all costs, even in the face of new credible data. Your strategy is one of influence and persuasion and not achieving this outcome feels like losing and a threat to your own credibility.

   Medium desire to win – you have a perspective and want it to be heard, but are open to alternative perspectives. You'll debate firmly but will reappraise in the face of strong new evidence.

   Low desire to win – you prioritize harmony over being right. Conflict feels risky and unproductive so you might quickly concede, even if you believe you have a valid point or data to share, to avoid tension.

The model shown in Figure 4 identifies six Conflict Styles. The six styles, plotted from left to right, are: Avoidant, Accommodating, Compromising, Collaborative, Inflexible and Aggressive.

Let's now look at each in turn

Avoidant: I avoid hard conversations altogether

The Avoidant style is made up of: Low conflict confidence + Low desire to win

If you identify as avoidant, you sidestep conflict wherever possible to protect yourself and others from what you perceive as the painful and irrecoverable nature of confrontation. You tell yourself 'bringing it up' is unlikely to achieve a good outcome and your best bet is to hope the issue will resolve itself without any intervention from you. You prioritize relationship harmony over being right or 'getting it right' in terms of the outcome.

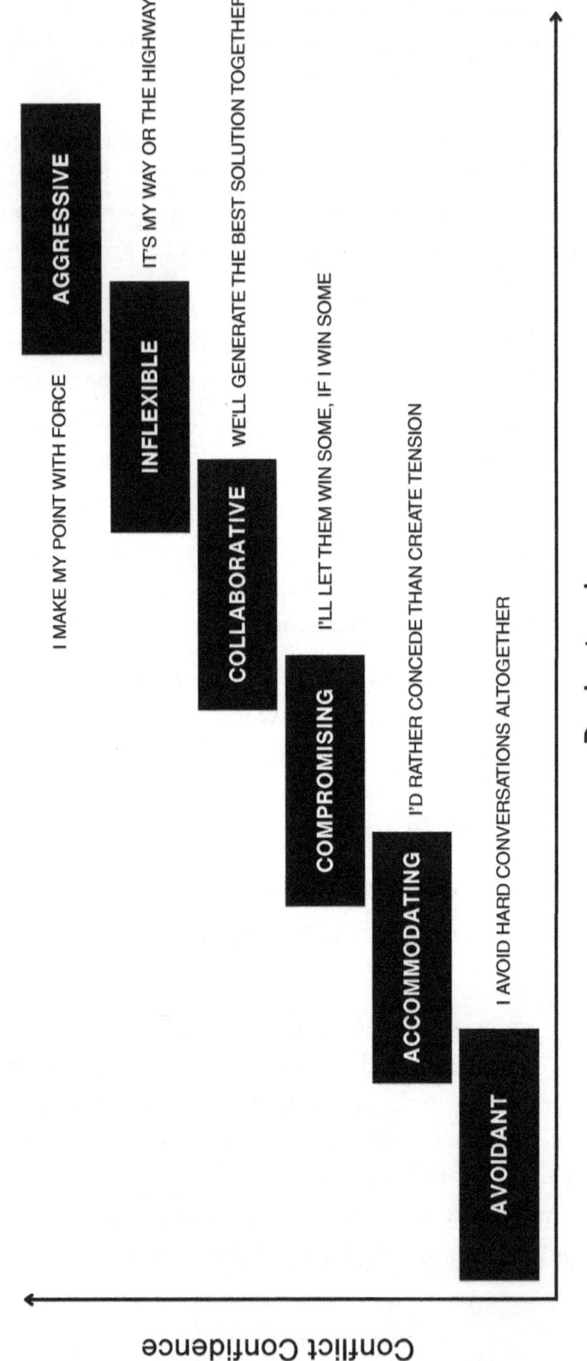

Figure 4: Default Conflict Style Model
Source: Driscoll & van Haarst, 2023

Sarah's story is very typical of what we hear in our Smart Conflict masterclasses. Sarah is a director in an insurance firm, and told us the following about her Avoidant default conflict style.

> *'I know I am avoidant. I have a team member right now who constantly misses deadlines. I know I should say something but I can't see them taking it well, so I'm stuck because I've been hoping it would resolve itself for six months. It's not getting any better, but it's hard to imagine that me simply saying "you need to start meeting deadlines" is suddenly going to magically make that happen. The problem is that even if I could tolerate missed deadlines, there is a very real impact on the rest of the team and I know they are frustrated about it'*

Accommodating: I'd rather concede than create tension

The accommodating style is made up of: Low conflict confidence + Low desire to win

An accommodating style prioritizes keeping the peace, even if it means your needs, the needs of the team or the needs relating to the task in hand (e.g. the project or business) are not met. Accommodating can be considered a form of Avoidance because although you do show up to the conversation, when you accommodate you are not centring what matters to you (the team or the business) or advocating for 'getting it right'. And just like the Avoidant style, you have little to no confidence that the relationship could survive any likely rupture caused by a confrontation.

Paul, a head of department at a Fintech business told us he often finds himself using an accommodating style with his CEO.

> *'For some reason when Jack asks me for feedback on his strategy, if I get the slightest sense that he might not appreciate the challenge I find myself quickly dismissing my concerns or questions and switch to prioritizing making sure he feels fully supported. The challenge is, when inevitably problems appear further down the line, I feel frustrated I didn't speak up and make sure the risks were known*

earlier when we might have actually been able to prevent some of the issues arising in the first place'

Compromising: I'll let them win some if I win some

The compromising style is made up of: Medium conflict confidence + Medium desire to win

The compromising style seeks to find a middle ground solution – we'll meet halfway, through mutual concessions. It presumes that the only alternative to having one winner and one loser is to split the wins and losses equally, or rests on a belief that this is the fairest way to move forward. You have enough confidence to express your needs and advocate for them on some level, and whilst your personal desire to win is tempered, your focus is on ensuring a fair solution (ensuring everyone gets the same) over finding the best solution – 'getting *it* right.'

Cara is the Head of Platforms at a broadcaster. Two departments that report to her were arguing over budget allocation, and both had presented strong cases that would benefit the business. Fairness is a core value of Cara's and it is important to her that she is perceived to treat others equally. So, instead of a deep discussion and needs-analysis on what budget is required by each to unlock specific outcomes, she split the available funds evenly, without fully understanding if that would result in neither team having the resources they needed to achieve each of their goals.

Collaborative: We'll generate the best solution together

The collaborative style is made up of: Medium conflict confidence + Medium desire to win

The collaborative style approaches disagreement with an open mind and a mindset that combines equal parts confidence (self-belief) and humility (awareness of your limitations). It prioritizes open, curious dialogue with a belief that the best solution may not as yet have been identified, and assumes that everyone involved in the conversation brings the capability and – between you – the perspectives and knowledge that are needed to get to a good solution. Collaborators believe that it is possible to achieve a win-win solution, because everyone is focused on the same shared goal to 'get it right', even if needs vary, or there are also additional individual goals at play.

Lars, Head of Distribution at an investment bank told us:

> *'I find taking a collaborative approach to agreeing terms with clients is the most effective style I've tried. I've realized that going in hard on how we want it to work doesn't make them feel we are trying to make things work for them. But equally when we've reluctantly agreed to terms that don't work for us, it's unravelled eventually. You know that saying "the client is always right"? I've found that doesn't really work in practice. So now I make sure I'm clear on where our red lines are, and really lean in to understand what matters most to them and then work on a case by case basis with them to get to something we can both tolerate long term and gets the best out of my team, which ultimately is what they want too'*

Inflexible: It's my way or the highway

The inflexible style is made up of: High conflict confidence + High desire to win

When we're inflexible, we're essentially communicating that we have already made up our mind coming into the conversation, and there is nothing we could discover during the course of the conversation that would change it, not even new, credible data. This style is characterized by a need for control and a dominant insistence that our proposed path is followed, sacrificing the relationship if necessary. We have a high level of certainty in our own perspective and ideas, and when we adopt this style we are valuing these above those of others. Those who default to the Inflexible style care very much about getting it right, but are sure that they *are right* (and that these are one and the same thing). Tonally, Inflexible sounds clear, firm but composed.

Many of our clients have given us examples of having to deliver inflexible messages to their organizations around policy changes, and many more have been on the receiving end of them. A common example of this has been the recent 'return to the office' mandates a number of businesses have chosen to deploy after a period of more flexible or hybrid working, with no exceptions. While Inflexibility is sometimes necessary when there is no room for negotiation, or urgency requires a fast and firm decision, there are plenty of other occasions where the Inflexible style is about winning, achieving this through limiting (which sometimes means silencing) other voices.

Aggressive: I make my point with force

The aggressive style is made up of: High conflict confidence + High desire to win

An aggressive style can be thought of as 'Inflexible Plus.' It contains all of the characteristics of the Inflexible style, but once we've moved into Aggressive it takes on an emotionally charged quality, and often contains a sense of high urgency. An aggressor will seek to be right at any and all expense to the relationship if necessary. Aggressive behaviours are often associated with a loss of control over our response. Making a point with force could mean raising our voices, sounding an alarm, using a low but intense tone, using threatening language, making ourselves physically intimidating, or unleashing strong feelings.

Max, a CTO in a gaming firm came to us for 1:1 coaching after some feedback he had received about his aggressive and combative style with his colleagues. What Max presented was an understanding on some level that he was upsetting people around him, but also a deep frustration at feeling misunderstood, a self-view as a direct 'straight talker,' and an assumption that in changing his style and taking the heat out of his interactions he would lose his impact and influence as a leader. He'd lose his 'edge.' He understood that people didn't like his aggressive style, but equally didn't see a good reason to change.

The six styles: Benefits and drawbacks

Our Default Conflict Style Model is so-called because of the pre-set, automatic response our genes, our personal histories and cultural experiences have shaped in us. But that is not to say that we behave in line with our default settings in all contexts, at all times. In fact, it's very likely that you have already learned to adapt your response depending on the situation you find yourself in, and the person you find yourself with. In our masterclasses we frequently hear from participants that '*how I show up is entirely situational*'. And to that we say, excellent! Because what we hope to achieve with the model is to help you identify the one or two most common instinctive styles you adopt, and to invite you to consider in what way these are working for you today, and where you might benefit from developing more situational flexibility. To be able to harness the very real pros of every single one of these styles and get to a place where you can choose the most appropriate style for the given situation. It's not useful to demonize *any* of the styles, as each has strengths in particular contexts.

We may have default 'autopilot' responses, but it's important to understand that conflict styles are not fixed personality traits; they are largely learned behaviours. This is hopefully encouraging, because it means we can learn and adopt new behaviours and styles if we want to, and if we are prepared to put the work in to get there.

Style guide: When to use which style

Table 1 shows you the best-use cases for each of the six conflict styles, and the contexts in which you should proceed with caution and consider flexing to a different approach.

Style fluidity

There's one final point we want to make about moving between styles. Not only is it smart to choose the most appropriate conflict style to meet the situation you are facing at any given moment – mastery of style flexibility also involves moving fluidly between styles during a single interaction, and/or deploying two styles at once, for example:

You start a conversation collaboratively, but don't feel you are getting anywhere, so you move to inflexibility and dictate what is going to happen next.

You start a conversation collaboratively, but don't feel you are getting anywhere so you switch to compromising or accommodating because it's not a high-stakes matter, and you want to focus on building the relationship right now.

You can even become adept at using multiple styles simultaneously, for example:

You decide to take a collaborative approach to a conversation to identify solutions, but will remain steadfast and inflexible about the problem needing a solution.

Identify your default conflict style

Carve out 15 minutes to do this exercise.

With the six default conflict styles in mind, answer the following questions in turn to help you identify the ones that you default to the most.

1) When I feel angry or frustrated my default style is…

   e.g. Avoidant/Aggressive/to try and get myself back to a Collaborative mindset

2) When someone else is visibly angry or frustrated I tend to…

   e.g. Avoid them/challenge them/help them/ignore them

3) When I know someone is avoiding conflict with me I tend to…

Table 1: Conflict style guide

Approach	Best-use cases	Be cautious if…
Avoidant	The other person is not in a place emotionally to productively engage with the topic (delay for now). You do not have all the data you need to have the conversation. You are not the best placed to have the conversation – someone else will get a better result. It's not the best use of your time, e.g. this is a low-stakes issue or a temporary one.	You risk not having a conversation that matters and won't be resolved without it. You're telling yourself you are being strategically avoidant, but you're using it as an excuse so you can avoid a conversation you don't want to have. You need to build trust in the relationship and open transparent lines of communication.
Accommodating	Trust and rapport need to be rebuilt, and accommodating the other person's request or view will not materially impact the task. Low-stakes decisions that will build goodwill and preserve your time and energy. Situations where you don't have (or are uncertain if you have) 'permission' to challenge.	Allowing them to 'be right' means you won't 'get it right,' which will have a significant impact on others or the task (for which you are in some way accountable). Not challenging or addressing issues now will mean you are simply storing up problems for later.

(Continued)

Table 1: (Continued)

Approach	Best-use cases	Be cautious if…
Compromising	When all other avenues have been exhausted and this is the only way to move out of stalemate, compromise can be a better solution than no solution. In time-sensitive situations where a 'good enough' solution will do (and that is what is on the table). In budget and financial negotiations, where this is often an expected approach and can lead to a win-win situation.	The end result means you will end up in a lose-lose situation with no one's needs being fully met. Saving time now might cost you time later, and the better choice is to keep going to find the right solution.
Collaborative	For complex or high-stakes decisions where alignment and buy-in are critical. When combining different data and perspectives on the same issue will help you get to the best answer. When you need to build trust. When you don't have positional power and you want someone else to do/change something – creating shared ownership is vital.	You need to move very fast (but watch out for using this as an excuse).

Approach	Best-use cases	Be cautious if…
Inflexible	When re-enforcing ethical, contractual or legal standards, being clear but firm is vital, e.g. safety policies or compliance requirements. When you need to communicate non-negotiable boundaries, e.g. company-wide mandates or important developmental performance feedback.	You don't have the full picture, and you risk not learning from the conversation about data and perspectives you haven't yet considered. Inflexibility will cause damage to a relationship that you don't want or can't afford. Your priority is to build psychological safety and to encourage diverse perspectives.
Aggressive	When urgent, high-stakes action is required, e.g. a life-or-death decision or action is needed; or you are confronting a serious behaviour breach where greater emotional force is needed to get it to stop in the moment (such as a fight). If you are operating in a culture where expressing yourself with emotional force is the expected norm and this might be the only way to be heard and get engagement (however, be cautious about assuming this is your *only* choice).	You are regularly resorting to an aggressive style. In 99% of cases adding an emotional force and intensity to your delivery is not going to make you land your message any more clearly; in fact it will do the opposite.

Source: The Power House, 2025

e.g. Join them in avoidance/challenge them/complain about them

4) I avoid conflict if…

   e.g. It's with someone senior/I don't think it will change anything/I'm worried I will say something I regret

5) I tend to accommodate when…

   e.g. It doesn't really matter/it's my boss/I'm tired/I've given up

6) If someone is clearly inflexible I will likely…

   e.g. Get aggressive/give in/call it out/dig my heels in

7) I can be inflexible about…

   e.g. Decisions that affect my team/my personal time/the things I enjoy

Now, take a moment to reflect on your answers:

What have you noticed about your answers?

What new insights do you have as a result of doing this exercise?

Understanding attachment styles in conflict

In Part 1 we introduce the idea that our origin stories shape how we show up and respond to conflict today. One way in which they do that is by informing our Attachment Style. Beginning in the 1950s, the behavioural psychologist John Bowlby researched the early bonds of babies and children with their caregivers. His work, and that of later psychologists Mary Ainsworth, Kim Bartholomew and Leonard Horowitz identified four core attachment styles: Secure, Anxious, Avoidant and Disorganized. Research indicates that our attachment style dictates how we handle intimacy, vulnerability and, of course, conflict.[4]

Here is a summary of the characteristics of each style:

Secure Attachment: Comfortable being close with others (intimacy) as they are alone (autonomous), generally trusting, emotionally available, and usually able to express their needs without guilt or drama. In conflict, securely attached people tend to believe that even though they are not always in sync, that others still care for them and that they are worthy of love. They tend to manage disagreements with calmness, open communication, and empathy, with a focus on trying to work it out. They are likely to be able to regulate their own emotions well.

Anxious Attachment (**Preoccupied**): Crave closeness but worry that the people they love will leave them (abandonment), and are often hypersensitive to potentially negative 'relationship cues' from others that indicate safety, emotional availability and reliability in relationships (e.g. they might get upset and worry someone is angry at them if they don't get a quick reply to a message). In conflict, Anxiously attached people may become emotional, clingy or demanding during disagreements. They tend to catastrophize and seek validation and reassurance both during and after a conflict and might feel they care more than others.

Avoidant Attachment (**Dismissive**): Value independence, and may struggle with emotional vulnerability and feel easily claustrophobic when people depend on them emotionally in relationships. Those with an Avoidant attachment style may find it hard to fully trust or open up with others, and they need space in relationships to feel like themselves – worrying that closeness will come at the cost of their freedom. In conflict, those with an avoidant attachment style can disappear, shut down or minimize problems. Conflict can feel overwhelming, leading to emotional detachment.

Disorganized Attachment (**Fearful-Avoidant**): Having a mix of anxious and avoidant tendencies, often stemming from unresolved trauma in childhood or early life, those with this attachment style crave closeness but fear being hurt or controlled. They often feel emotionally overwhelmed in relationships and struggle to fully trust others. In conflict, those with a disorganized attachment style are likely to oscillate between emotional outbursts and withdrawal, creating unpredictable conflict patterns which they feel unable to break out of.

Understanding your own attachment style and that others may have differing styles to yours can help give you context as to why some colleagues (or indeed anyone around you) may react very differently to the same situation.

Reading through the above and reflecting on when and how you've experienced a charged emotional reaction or discomfort in a hard conversation or conflict – e.g. feeling ignored, criticized or misunderstood – can you begin to identify how your own attachment patterns might show up? Do you tend to lean in, withdraw or shut down? What assumptions do you often make about yourself and other people in tense moments? And what insight can this offer?

Illuminating conflict dynamics

The first two exercises have been designed to support you to reflect on how you show up in conflict scenarios in general. The rest of this chapter introduces models that can help you better understand what is going on in relationship dynamics where conflict is already present, or following a specific confrontation you may have been in. We urge you to come back to the *Reflection* 'R' not just to prepare for a hard conversation where relations are currently good, but also after a rupture or run-in, to reflect on what just happened and prepare your next Smart Conflict move.

What are we *actually* fighting about?

A lot of what makes a hard conversation hard is about knowing you are going to land some unpopular news or some potentially unpalatable observations. But sometimes it's not the first time you're having the conversation, or you've felt your interactions with an individual or group of people are increasingly tricky and fractious and before you know it, you would characterize the relationship as 'in conflict'.

So what can we do once it's happened? Head to the *Repair* chapter for a full rundown on what to do after a rupture (e.g. a tense exchange, or 'falling out' of some kind), but this next reflection exercise could help you make sense of what's really going on under the surface of the conflict, and give you some clues on how to be smart about what you do next.

A key feature of those relationships that can successfully move from rupture to repair is the ability to identify and recognize the root cause or deeper issue that has triggered the surface argument. When we're not able to do this, the unidentified issue remains, hidden under the surface and hardening positions over time.

Couples Therapy Researcher Howard Markman identified the three key themes that conflicts are typically rooted in. They provide a useful way to help you triage and better understand the unmet needs at play in your conflicts. Note that overlap of themes is common – more than one can be in play. Below is a summary of the three themes.

Power and control: *Do I have autonomy?*

When we are fighting about power and control we might feel we are wrestling with feelings about whose priorities matter the most, or who is making the big decisions. Maybe we are arguing about who works harder, or who has the most senior client relationships. When this need is unmet we will likely feel controlled and powerless, to which we might respond with resistance, frustration or passive-aggression.

We might think and feel things along the lines of:

> *'You constantly override my decisions in meetings without consulting me.'*
>
> *'Because I'm junior to you, I feel like I have to get your approval for everything, even when it's within my job description.'*

'You always decide the project timelines without asking for my input.'

Care and closeness: *Do you care about me?*

When our conflict is centred around care and closeness, there is tension because it feels like the other person doesn't care about us personally, beyond our job title. Without care and closeness, we may feel rejected, unworthy or insecure, leading to behaviours such as seeking excessive validation or, conversely, withdrawal.

We might think and feel things along the lines of:

'Why can't you back me up in meetings when I'm under pressure instead of criticizing me afterwards?'

'Why am I always the one following up on our collaboration? I feel like I'm doing all the chasing.'

'Why don't we check in more often as a team? I feel disconnected from you and the group.'

Respect and recognition: *Do you value my contribution?*

This third theme is centred on our need for validation and self-worth. Perhaps we feel someone else is taking all the credit for our work, or not recognizing or valuing our contribution to the project. When we don't feel this need is being met, we might feel inadequate or disrespected, behave defensively or overcompensate to prove ourselves.

We might think and feel things along the lines of:

'You take credit for ideas we developed together.'

'You rarely acknowledge my contributions to the project in front of leadership.'

'I don't think you realize how often I step in to handle client issues quietly behind the scenes.'

When one of these three needs goes unmet, we have a breeding ground for misunderstandings and unhealthy conflict. By identifying and acknowledging which needs are in play we can ensure we are having the right conversation about the right problem and move towards resolving the conflict and repairing the relationship.

Case study: Resolving a co-founder conflict by surfacing unmet needs

Two co-founders of an early stage tech startup, Alex and Jordan, came to us when they found themselves locked in a bitter dispute over who should take the role of CEO and who should become COO. Not only did they both feel strongly about taking the CEO role, but on paper there wasn't an obvious and clear-cut answer about who would be the better candidate. Alex had extensive experience in strategy and operations, while Jordan excelled in fundraising and team management. Both felt they could bring a lot to the CEO role, and they felt equally entitled to it. When we met them, things were tense and awkward and the discussion around the role was getting in the way of them getting on with building the business.

Taking them through our *Conflict Wayfinder* process (an intensive resolution intervention that combines techniques from Mediation, Executive Coaching and Smart Conflict), we supported them to explore their deeper motivations and unmet needs to see if this could help generate new insight and help them get unstuck. Alex realized that his desire to be CEO stemmed from a desire for power and control over the company's growth strategy, and shared a concern that unless he was in the CEO role he would not be the ultimate decision maker when it mattered. He admitted, 'If I'm honest, I do want to be in charge. The idea that I would play second fiddle in the company I'm putting so much into building is hard for me to swallow.' Meanwhile, Jordan's push for the CEO role stemmed from the fact that he had successfully secured all their investment to date, with an assumption that this would automatically be the deciding factor. He didn't feel Alex recognized the critical nature of his contribution, without which, he told him emphatically 'there would *be no company*'.

By identifying these unmet needs, the pair could focus their energy and discussions exactly where they needed to – not on who most deserved to be or was most skilled to take on the CEO role, but on what the shared remit for the CEO and COO might be around strategy, and how Alex could demonstrate more recognition for the value that Jordan brought from fundraising. In the end, Jordan became the CEO: the pair realigned their decision criteria for the role as being focused on external optics and fundraising efforts, while ensuring that key strategic decisions would always be agreed together. Crucially, they agreed to regular role reviews, to make sure that the needs of the business were always the driving force behind key decisions.

By addressing their underlying emotional drivers, Alex and Jordan shifted from ego-driven conflict – the need to 'win' by getting their own personal needs met – to a solution that leveraged their strengths to meet the needs of the business – ultimately strengthening their partnership.

Unmet needs mapping

This is an exercise you can use to self-reflect, or you might choose to do it together with the person who you are having a disagreement with, to see if it unlocks the underlying issues.

Whether this exercise will be productive in a pair depends on the quality of your relationship at the time. If it's fractious between you, digging further under the surface may risk an escalation, so go gently. Also be mindful that different people have different appetites for self-disclosure – one client told us she would '*rather put live bees under my eyelids*' than have this kind of conversation. However if your relationship is generally on a solid footing and you are both open to reflection, it can be very effective in getting to a solution that works for you both.

This exercise takes 10 minutes alone, or around 30 minutes when done in a pair.

With the three themes described above in mind reflect then note down:

a) On a scale of 1 to 10, how important are each of the themes to you personally?

b) How far are each of those needs being met in the context of this particular relationship? Which of them are not being met, and how?

If you are working in a pair, note your answers and then discuss and compare them in turn and see what themes emerge. If you are reflecting on your own, note down your own rating from 1 to 10, then make some informed hypotheses about which unmet needs the other person may be bringing into the relationship. Think about how these might be informing how you interact together.

Then looking at your answers, explore alone or together:

c) What clues are there about the underlying unmet needs for both of you?

d) What insights do these offer about what you could both do to help recognize and/or meet these needs, for yourself and for each other?

e) What could *you* commit to doing or experimenting with? What requests do you have for the other person? What other actions could you take (for things in your direct control and for things which may need the support or involvement of others)?

Stepping out of the drama triangle

The next model we want to share with you is one that many of our clients have found incredibly illuminating when trying to make sense of, and break out of, tricky dynamics with their colleagues.

Developed by Stephen Karpman in 1968, the Drama Triangle identifies three roles people unconsciously play in a conflict: the Victim, the Persecutor and the Rescuer.[5] It's rooted in Transactional Analysis, a framework first introduced in the 1960s by psychiatrist Eric Berne that can help us understand how we are showing up and explore the dynamics between other people when we are in conflict (for more on Transactional Analysis see Berne's seminal 1964 book *Games People Play: The Psychology of Human Relationships*).[6]

The Victim, Persecutor and Rescuer roles are not fixed positions or identities, but roles we move fluidly between, going from point-to-point on the metaphorical triangle, even during the course of one conversation.

The Victim is characterized by feeling powerless and helpless. We feel we've been unfairly treated and positioned at a disadvantage, often leaving us feeling resentment and lacking control in the situation.

The Persecutor seeks to control and have power in the situation, usually with dominance, aggression and criticism, pointing the finger of blame squarely at others.

The Rescuer gravitates towards a caretaker role in order to have a sense of control and superiority, offering unsolicited help with the aim to reduce others' suffering. This involves crossing boundaries, and being overly involved.

In dysfunctional interactions, you and your counterparts in conflict can shift your position between these three roles, upping the drama each time. So you can start off feeling the victim, making sure everyone in the meeting knows how put-upon you feel and how unfair it all is. Then, you can become frustrated, and make demands about what will happen next, seeking to control the outcome. When someone becomes upset in response to what's happening you can then rush in with the tissues, demonstrating what a nice person you are *really* (and the drama wasn't your fault at all, you're just trying to help everyone else, of course...), and so it goes on.

However, we all know people who have default positions they adopt no matter the day or the conversation. Perhaps you recognize in the description of the *Victim* role a colleague who struggles with assertiveness and is endlessly dependent on others, all whilst feeling miserably stuck and at the mercy of circumstance. Or maybe you recognize in yourself or others a lack of empathy and a tendency to criticize that can translate into a *Persecutor* stance. Or, you may have the self-awareness to know you have an irresistible urge to rush in and *rescue* or 'sort things out' for other people, perhaps having hard conversations on their behalf, making excuses for their behaviour, or doing work for them when it's not your responsibility. None of these roles is healthy, and ultimately we want to step off the drama triangle and into what Eric Berne called an Adult stance. The *Adult* position is aligned with rational thought, emotional regulation and present-moment awareness. It leaves the drama at the door, relies on objective data and brings in perspectives grounded in past experiences.

The drama triangle allows us to see with more clarity the underlying motivations and patterns driving conflicts, and with this awareness, we can choose to step out of our unhelpful roles into something more empowering in the next conversation. So, if in reflecting on a series of recent interactions with someone, or a group of people, you notice that you are caught up in the drama triangle, here's what to do next.

In his 2005 book *The Power of TED (The Empowerment Dynamic)*,[7] David Emerald offered some smarter roles to try out instead:

Shift from **Victim** to **Creator**: asserting your own needs and taking the agency to solve problems, not just identify them.

Shift from **Persecutor** to **Challenger**: offering assertive but constructive feedback that is no longer an emotionally charged attack (see the *Readiness* chapter on giving effective feedback).

Shift from **Rescuer** to **Coach**: providing empathy, whilst encouraging the other person to find their own solutions.

Breaking free from the drama triangle requires self-awareness (yes – this *is* the key to everything), and a commitment to choose to step out of it and into more productive and constructive roles, ones where we accept responsibility for our positions without asserting power over others.

The drama triangle roles are intertwined and co-dependent as we shift roles in response to others in the moment. When a colleague arrives at a meeting in full persecution mode, doling out the criticisms and laying the blame squarely at our door, our instinctive response will be to take on the Victim position because the persecutor *needs* a victim to persecute. If they were able to shift into the challenger role, they would immediately give the victim agency and control, paving the way for the victim to move into the creator role – a victim needs a persecutor after all, so without one, the victim role dissolves. Any rescuers also become redundant (who is there to rescue now?). By changing just one role in the triangle, we can change all the roles.

Drama triangle diagnostic

This exercise takes 15 minutes.

Here are four questions to support your self-reflection based on the drama triangle. Think about a conflict you have experienced and answer:

1) Which role(s) did I find myself stepping into during this conflict – Victim, Persecutor or Rescuer? What emotions drove that response?
2) Did I unintentionally reinforce someone else's role in the drama triangle? How might I have invited or escalated those dynamics?
3) What would a healthier response have looked like if I had approached the situation from an empowered, accountable stance instead?
4) What could I do differently in the future?

Unpacking trust

A breakdown of trust can make all conversations feel hard. In his book *The Trust Equation*,[8] David Maister identified a formula for the key elements that build or destroy trust.

Trust = (Credibility + Reliability + Intimacy) ÷ Self-Orientation

Trust is highest, therefore, with those people who we believe to be credible (we think they are competent at their jobs), reliable (they do what they say they will consistently), with whom we share a level of intimacy (I can confide in them without fear) and finally, who we don't find self-orientated (they're not overly focused on their own needs/agenda over the group needs).

This formula highlights that being trustworthy isn't just about being skilled or dependable; it's also about fostering secure, authentic relationships while minimizing self-interest (or the appearance of self-interest, anyway). The equation offers a practical lens for diagnosing why trust might have been reduced or lost in a relationship, as well as a framework for identifying where to focus efforts to rebuild it.

Complete a trust audit

Take five minutes to reflect on the following three questions:

1) Think of someone you don't entirely trust. Where in the equation is the gap that is contributing to the issue?
2) Now flip it. If they were looking at this equation, what would they say is the gap in the way you are showing up for them?
3) What's one step you could take towards rebuilding trust, now?

For more detailed strategies on how to rebuild trust see the chapter on *Repair*.

Projection in conflict: When it's not about them (but it feels like it is)

> *'We don't see things as they are, we see them as we are.'*
> – Anaïs Nin

First identified by Freud – the father of psychoanalysis – in the late 1800s, projection is a psychological defence mechanism leading us to unconsciously attribute our own feelings, thoughts or traits to someone else.[9] In simple terms, a defence mechanism is a way our mind automatically protects us from uncomfortable thoughts, feelings or stress. In conflict, this means we may see our own fears, insecurities or negative qualities in another person – without realizing they actually come from within us. The target of this projection may in reality have entirely different motivations, emotions or ideas but we are blinded by the picture we are projecting onto them, often driven by a sense of threat or fear (see the *Regulation* chapter for more on the threat response).

As an illustration, we once mediated a dispute between Ben, a management consultant, and Kate, the founder of the boutique consultancy he was working for. While clearly ambitious, Ben presented as anxious about his status in relation to the rest of the delivery team. It soon became clear that while he wanted to take the lead with clients… he didn't want the associated workload. It came to a head when Ben tried to forcefully 'delegate' all the grunt work of a project to another member of the team, but while still taking the credit, and the fee. When Kate discovered this and challenged him, Ben became furious, claiming: '*You are so dominant! You want to control everything! My contribution is never recognized!*' Instead of recognizing how his own dominant and undermining behaviour was affecting the team, Ben projected these characteristics onto Kate, in an attempt to protect his self-image and save face. Unable to accept his part in the dispute, Ben quit – holding firm to his version of events and choosing to preserve his pride, rather doing the uncomfortable work of taking responsibility for his actions.

As many a pun-loving teacher has said before us, 'to assume makes an ass of you and me.' When we assume we know what is on another person's mind rather than asking them straight, or testing multiple theories as to what is going on, we often get it seriously, embarrassingly (occasionally career-endingly) wrong. In Cognitive Behaviour Therapy this is known as 'mind-reading' and taught as one of the major thinking traps to overcome to react more skillfully to conflict and stress. We quite simply cannot read other people's minds. While many people would argue we should rely on 'gut feelings' alone, your gut can be confused by stress hormones and doesn't always have access to the information that would convince your brain to think again, rather than acting on projections.

In a conflict at work, projection might look like:

a) Blaming others for our feelings: instead of admitting we feel insecure, we accuse someone of criticizing us too much.

   Example: If you are feeling guilty about being unhelpful, you might say, '*You never support me!*'

b) Seeing our own traits in others: we may find certain behaviours especially irritating in others because they mirror our own weaknesses. One of our university lecturers introduced us to the idea of 'if you spot it, you got it!' which – while perhaps not scientific – is a good reminder to check in on potential projection when we feel particularly annoyed with someone.

   Example: A boss who is disorganized may harshly criticize an employee for being '*chaotic and forgetful.*'

c) Misinterpreting intentions: we can unconsciously apply our own responses to others. So, if we tend to be jealous, we may assume others are envious of us when it's not the case.

   Example: A colleague feels threatened by competition but insists, '*You're always trying to outshine me.*'

Projection check-in tool

The questions below have been designed to help you identify if projection is in play in your thinking.

Thinking of a live or recent conflict take five minutes to reflect on the following three questions:

1) Am I reacting more strongly than the situation warrants?
2) Am I assuming motives without clear evidence?
3) Does this behaviour remind me of past experiences or insecurities?

Creating a reflection habit

In this chapter we have introduced you to a number of models, tools and exercises all designed to support you to increase your self-awareness of your default conflict style, your instinctive responses and the roles you might play, as well as diagnostics that can help you analyse a conflict you are already in, including identifying the hidden unmet needs behind it.

It's this self-awareness that will enable you to know where you are today, decide where you ideally want to be and then make a plan to move in the right direction (and the rest of this book will help you with how to do that).

Keeping a reflection journal is a great way to build self-awareness and is also proven to support sustained behaviour change. Through the regular practice of reflecting back over your meeting, your day, week or year, and making a point of noticing and recording your observations about how you showed up, and what you plan to do differently next time, will form new connections between your neurons – the process of neuroplasticity, literally the brain changing itself – until what was once new and forced becomes your automatic and effortless operating mode.[10]

We've designed the journal below to make building this habit into your week as easy as possible.

Conflict reflection journal

We'd recommend allocating 10 minutes each week to ask yourself the following questions and suggest choosing a regular time to do this (e.g. every Friday on your commute home) and put it in your diary as this is more likely to help you form a consistent reflection habit.

1) **When did I feel strong emotions this week?** (e.g. anger, frustration, sadness, jealousy, happiness, excitement)
2) **What hard conversations did I have this week?**
3) **What happened?** Describe the stimulus event for each one – why did you choose to have the conversation? Was it planned or spontaneous?
4) **How did I respond?** What did you do, say and feel?
5) **How did the other person respond?** What did they say or do in response? What emotions did they show or express?
6) **What does that tell me about what I care about and is important to me?** Which of your core values was demonstrated or threatened?
7) **What does it tell me about what the other person cares about?** What evidence do you have for this? What can you learn from this?
8) **How does caring about this benefit the team or organization I am part of?** (e.g. 'They can always rely on me to tell the truth')
9) **How is caring about this a potential pitfall for my team or organization?** (e.g. 'I might be perceived as negative')
10) **My learning from this reflection is...**
11) **I will take the following action/s to implement this new learning...**

Reflection summary

- **Self-reflection is the starting point for changing how we show up in conflict.**
- **Your default conflict style is shaped by genetic, early family and cultural experiences and awareness of it is key to choosing more effective responses.**
- **There are six conflict styles. They aren't fixed personality traits but approaches we can learn which can and should be adapted depending on the context.**
- **Unmet emotional needs (e.g. for power, for care, for recognition) are often the hidden fuel behind workplace conflict.**
- **We can unconsciously adopt unhelpful 'drama' roles in conflicts and need to learn to identify them and step into more constructive 'empowering' ones.**
- **Trust is made up of a number of elements. We need to know where to focus to rebuild it consciously and effectively.**
- **Regular reflection is the lever that turns insight into lasting behavioural change.**

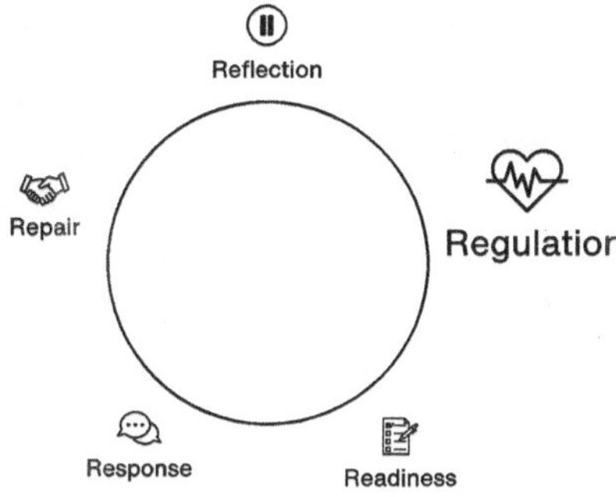

6
Regulation

'Between stimulus and response there is a space. In that space is our power to choose our response. In our response lies our growth and our freedom.'– Viktor Frankl[1]

'I don't know what happened. I didn't plan to, but before I knew it, I was up from my desk, in Roberta's office and telling her off for the disrespect of cancelling on me yet again! Then – perhaps even worse – I burst into tears and had to run out in front of everyone on the floor.

Yes, her repeated rescheduling of the project meetings was annoying me, but I'm just not the type of person that loses it at work. I'm usually very even tempered. I apologized later once I'd calmed down, but I'm mortified. What's wrong with me at the moment?'

Helen, a highly productive and experienced programme manager for a tech consulting firm, was put forward for coaching to get some support after she seemed to be struggling with the pressures of a recent promotion. Always a cheerful, stalwart, star performer in her 10 years of service, for the first time in her career she had started showing signs of stress and experiencing emotional outbursts that were very out of character. The focus of our work became giving Helen strategies to notice her 'state' (how she was thinking and feeling moment to moment) and then to select techniques to regulate herself, i.e. to get into a frame of mind (and body) that would allow her to choose a considered response, rather than to react automatically from a place of strong emotion and regret it later.

Put simply, self-regulation refers to the ability to consciously manage our thoughts, emotions and behaviours. It's whatever we do with our minds and bodies (e.g. self-talk, deep breathing, vigorous exercise, mindfulness) when we're trying to calm down, to cheer up, or to 'get in the zone' – whatever that particular zone needs to be. Clients are often surprised at the degree to which coaching (whether that's leadership, high performance or conflict coaching) includes a focus on self-regulation. That is, managing *themselves* – as much as, or even more than, managing others.

The ability to self-regulate effectively is one of the most foundational skills in leadership (and in life). If we can lead *ourselves* well, we can speak and act from a place that reflects our true values, and lead others – whether that is a team of 200 salespeople or our fractious two-year-old – in a way that is calm, considered and kind.

It's worth noting that stress responses are highly individual, and we would invite you as part of your reflections on your Default Conflict Settings (see the exercises in the *Reflection* chapter) to think now about what your personal triggers are, and how reactive you tend to be in particular contexts. For example, we often behave differently at work in the face of stress or conflict than we do at home. There can be some people that just get under our skin whatever they do, whereas others can do exactly the same things and we are totally unmoved – perhaps even amused – by the behaviour.

Our triggers can also be heightened by environmental or situational factors. You might know that you are more short-tempered or prone to tears if you haven't slept enough, if you're hungry (hangry), anxious, overwhelmed, frustrated, bored... we all have our own *thing*. If we can become aware of what it is, then we can take steps to manage our environment and responses to compensate and give ourselves a better chance of being our best selves in a hard conversation.

Some people are naturally less prone to stress – you know, the friend who is so relaxed she's almost horizontal – and therefore it takes a lot more for them to be triggered to react. Some people will already be highly skilled at self-regulation and have practices they regularly use – we're looking at the yoga enthusiasts and meditators among you. But we all have our limits. And it's at times of unusual stress and pressure, or at moments of unexpected conflict, that it's very helpful to know how to get ourselves back to a place of rational calm quickly.

In this chapter we're going to explain a little of how the human stress response works and share some techniques you can experiment with to self-regulate when you need to. Some of us struggle a great deal with self-regulation and are prone to reactivity, and if that's you, please have compassion for yourself. It can be hard. There are many reasons we might struggle to manage our reactions to stress including, but not limited to: the individual differences of genetics, past trauma, neurodiversity, adverse life events, brain age and hormonal states at different life stages. The good news is that, with the right practices, we can improve our ability to choose our responses in the moment – even if that choice is simply to remove yourself politely from the situation to calm down and return to it another time.

You can choose your response

When we teach self-regulation in workshops, many participants are surprised by the language we use – such as 'choosing your response' and 'choosing your thoughts' – and the idea that it is even possible (or in some cases, even desirable) to be more deliberate and measured about our words and actions in the moment. We often hear phrases such as:

> *'But this is just who I am – I've always been like this. Can I really do anything about it?'*
>
> *'I* am *an emotional person but that's how I get things done – it's part of my style and my team understands that. If I change how I communicate I'll be less effective.'*
>
> *'I don't want to be robotic or come across as trying to be something I'm not – authenticity is one of my core values.'*
>
> *'Is it really possible to manage your thoughts? They just happen to me!'*

Most of us won't have been taught in childhood how our amazing brains work or the fundamentals of how to manage our tricky emotions, so it's understandable that these skills are still brand new to many of the adults we work with in our Smart Conflict programmes. For some participants, the realization that their automatic emotional responses are having a major, often negative, impact on the people around them is a new and sometimes unwelcome discovery.

However, the *very* good news is that it's never too late to start. This can be a huge subject, and if you are intrigued or feel you need more help in this area, we've included a list of further recommended reading on neuroscientific theory and practical self-help in *Further Resources*. As ever, if you feel like your emotions are getting the better of you and you don't know where to start – please don't suffer in silence and do seek support.

A bit about the brain's stress response

We are not neuroscientists, but in our work on Smart Conflict we often start by sharing a few of the core concepts of how we as humans respond to stress and other kinds of perceived threat, and how this might show up in your behaviour. Below is a whistle-stop tour of some of the key terminology you may have encountered, and that we will refer to later in this book.

The 'Three Fs' of the stress response – fight, flight or freeze

In the 1920s the psychologist Walter Cannon first described 'fight, flight and freeze' responses as a key part of the human acute stress response, and these are the most often referenced and worked with today in coaching and therapy.[2] However, in 2000 psychologist Shelley Taylor and her colleagues identified an alternative reaction – the 'tend and befriend' response to stress, which performs quite a different and potentially more useful function.[3] As you read these descriptions, notice which of these responses you have experienced, and if there is one that tends to happen more than others when you are in stressful situations.

Fight

Our brain's amygdala is like an ancient alarm system, always on the lookout for signs of danger and threats to our survival. When it detects a threat it sends a signal that releases stress hormones like adrenaline and cortisol, preparing your body for action. The problem is that while the risk of being eaten by a sabre-tooth tiger today is precisely zero, the amygdala often perceives mundane everyday stressors as 'threats' – e.g. a tense exchange with a colleague, a looming presentation, or overwhelming to-do list – leading to overreactions or outbursts that may not serve you well.

The Fight response arises when we feel threatened and react – consciously or not – to confront the perceived danger. In practice this might look like frustration, anger or the need to assert control. If you've ever felt the urge to argue or 'push back' in a tense situation, that's your fight response at work. While this reaction can serve us when we need to stand up for ourselves in situations of danger or real threat, in most everyday interactions (including at work) an aggressive or argumentative communication style in response to stress will tend to lead to an escalation of tensions – especially if the other person's 'fight' response is activated in return. People who tend to be hot headed when stressed can create environments that feel less psychologically safe for the people around them. You might feel better for getting it all off your chest… but it's unlikely anyone else will. Those who place themselves on the Aggressive end of the conflict scale (see the *Reflection* chapter) will probably be triggered most frequently into the Fight response in reaction to a conflict or unexpected hard conversation.

Flight

The Flight response is about escape, manifesting as an urge to avoid the situation altogether. In modern life this could mean procrastinating to avoid a conversation or task we are dreading, ignoring an uncomfortable issue, or simply leaving a conversation or environment that feels stressful. While Flight is undeniably the right choice in genuinely unsafe scenarios (and in some circumstances when a hard conversation isn't going well – see the chapter on *Response*) it can also prevent us from addressing difficult but important things, stop us reaching goals which are important to our sense of achievement, or completing tasks essential to our job performance. Those who place themselves on the Avoidant end of the conflict scale will probably be triggered most frequently into the Flight response in reaction to a conflict or unexpected hard conversation.

Freeze

The Freeze response, sometimes described as feeling petrified (literally 'turned to stone') or in more mundane circumstances just stuck, happens when neither fight nor flight seems like a viable option. This response can lead to a sense of paralysis – making you feel powerless or unable to act. In these moments, you might stay silent and still to avoid drawing attention to yourself, be unable to make decisions, lose motivation, or experience a sense of detachment from the situation you are in.[4] As with the other responses, in times of real threat, not making any sudden moves and taking steps to make yourself as invisible as possible can be protective. There are some circumstances in a work-based conflict when saying and doing nothing in the moment can be a good course of action (see the chapter on *Response*). But in most cases a prolonged lack of action will just keep us stuck somewhere we don't want to be. Those who tend to be Accommodating on the conflict scale are likely to freeze in the face of hard conversation, taking the path of least resistance, which is often giving in to the most forceful voice.

Tend and befriend

The Tend and Befriend response is about social bonding, caregiving and cooperation in the face of stress. Shelley Taylor's research indicates that tend and befriend behaviours are evolutionary mechanisms aimed at improving survival through social connection and nurturing, particularly in situations of threat. This response is partly mediated by the hormone oxytocin, often called the bonding hormone. Oxytocin plays a key role in the creation of trust and empathy, and it increases in both men and women under stress, although studies suggest it may have a more pronounced effect on social behaviour in women.

While the fight, flight or freeze responses are heavily driven by adrenaline and cortisol, oxytocin helps calm the stress response and promotes prosocial behaviours like forming alliances.[5] In this way, the reflex to tend and befriend can serve as a protective mechanism, helping individuals form supportive networks to buffer the effects of perceived threats and stressful times. If you identified yourself as most often landing on Compromising or Collaborative on the conflict scale you may often default to tend and befriend in the face of stress. While this might seem the most desirable of the four responses we've described here, there's an important caveat – in an effort to keep the peace Tend and Befriend can tip into people-pleasing or lead to poor decision making driven by a desire to appease both 'sides' of a conflict, rather than working on the best solution to the problem.

How to self-regulate

So now you know what happens in your body and mind when you feel stressed by your circumstances or a potential conflict is on the horizon, what do you do to get yourself back into a calm, rational state that allows you to make conscious choices about your words and behaviour?

There are a lot of different techniques available, and we use many of them in our coaching work and in our own lives, too. We find it helps to put them into two broad categories: Top-Down practices and Bottom-Up practices:

Top-Down practices are what we call thinking based, which often involve observing your thoughts, challenging or replacing unhelpful ones, and creating a more helpful and compassionate inner soundtrack of inner thoughts.

Bottom-Up practices are what we call body-based – working with breathing, physical awareness and types of movement which help to calm the nervous system.

Some people find Top-Down techniques most effective, others Bottom-Up. The practices that work for you will be very individual, and we invite you to try a variety and see what's most helpful, and what's less effective for you. There is no right or wrong in terms of which techniques to use in what circumstances, but we find that sometimes it helps to match the technique to the presenting symptoms of stress.

If your mind is in an overdrive of negative self-talk, or you find yourself caught in a doom-spiral of 'what if?'s then a Top-Down, thinking-based technique might be the first thing to try. If you are experiencing unpleasant physical sensations related to stress – e.g. butterflies or a sinking feeling in the stomach, tightness in the chest, nervous trembling, a general sense of panic – then a Bottom-Up body-based technique might be the quickest way to start getting some relief.

There are many different types and versions of these techniques, and your personal prescription will be unique to you. It would be impossible to include them all here, but below we're describing some of the most popular, evidence-based techniques we use in our practice.

When to regulate

As with most new habits, practising your techniques little and often throughout your week is more effective than an occasional long session. What works best in our experience is to develop a mix of go-to in-the-moment techniques that can help you to quickly calm down when you need to, and 'maintenance' practices which you build into your weekly routine that increase your overall sense of well-being, and lead to a more regulated nervous system for the long term.

In terms of how to use *Regulation* in the context of Smart Conflict and hard conversations at work, we would recommend finding practices that you can use *before* (to get into a calm, well-regulated mindset), *during* (to help you hold your nerve and/or stay calm in the face of an unexpected development) and *after* (to recover from the conversation before you go into the rest of your day, if necessary, and/or to reassure yourself of a job well done).

An example 'prescription' drawn from the techniques described in detail below could be:

Before:

- In the days and/or hours before the hard conversation, use **positive self-talk** to maintain your confidence and offer yourself the support of your own **compassionate inner voice**.
- Practise **cadence breathing (3-3-6)** for 10 minutes twice a day to calm your nervous system (say, on your commute, or during breaks between meetings), or for a few rounds whenever you notice you are feeling worried or anxious.
- If you find yourself distracted by anticipation or on autopilot ruminating on 'what if's, bring yourself back into the present moment using the **5-4-3-2-1 Mindful Noticing Technique**.

During:

- If you are finding the conversation stressful, find a reason to take a pause (e.g. excuse yourself to use the loo, or to grab a glass of water, or take a moment to make both of you a hot drink). While out of the room, take deep, **mindful breaths**, notice your thoughts and '**unhook**' from anything unhelpful.
- If you don't want or need to leave the room but are struggling with rising emotions, use a **grounding technique** (such as just noticing the sensation of your feet on the floor), or screw up and release your toes inside your shoes, noticing the physical sensation.
- At any point you need to soothe yourself you can discreetly use the **Physiological Sigh**. You can leave the room to do this, but it's perfectly possible to do in the moment without being obvious, just don't make the in or out breaths too big or pronounced – you can practise this in advance with a friend observing if you want reassurance it's not noticeable (Louise sometimes uses this if she's feeling nervous presenting in front of a roomful of people and no one has ever mentioned it, yet!)

After:

- Whatever happened during the conversation, first of all tap into that reassuring compassionate inner voice – you did it! Remind yourself of everything you did well or that you felt was successful. Once you've taken this step, you can reflect on what you would do differently next time or consider any actions you need to take – but it's important not to beat yourself up or focus solely on the negative (this can trigger you into fight, flight or freeze meaning that your next actions come from a dysregulated rather than rational and considered place).

- If you are feeling stressed or anxious, take a few minutes to use one of your go-to techniques to calm yourself; breathing practices can be the most accessible here (some clients go and hide in the loo and breathe for five minutes, before emerging recomposed and swan-like to attend their next meeting).
- Make time as soon as you can for one of your maintenance practices such as **HIIT exercises** or **mindfulness** to support the elimination of built-up adrenaline and cortisol from your body and provide a sense of overall well-being.

Top-Down techniques

ACT – unhooking from unhelpful thoughts

Acceptance and Commitment Therapy (known as ACT) is a strongly evidence-based, cognitive behavioural intervention that helps people develop 'psychological flexibility' by learning to accept their thoughts and emotions instead of struggling with them, while committing to actions that align with their personal values. Developed by Steven C. Hayes in the 1980s, ACT combines elements of mindfulness and behaviour change strategies to help people live happier and more meaningful lives, even in the presence of difficult thoughts or emotions.[6]

Unhooking is one of many helpful techniques for thought management and self-regulation. You can use it when you notice yourself 'hooked onto' a negative, anxiety-inducing or self-critical thought that's getting in the way of you doing something you need or want to do. Many of us spend a large part of our daily lives going round and round the same habitual thought loops. According to 2024 research, not everyone has an inner voice. Somewhere between 70% and 90% of the general population experience their thoughts as an inner monologue, and 5 to 10%

experience thoughts instead through images, feelings or other non-verbal forms of cognition.[7]

ACT theory would say that by the time we reach adulthood many (indeed most) of our thoughts occur automatically, triggered by cues in our environment and in our bodies. We've probably all had the experience of unexpectedly coming across a particular smell – e.g. a perfume, cut grass, wood smoke, a particular food cooking – and immediately been transported back to a time, place or person connected to it in our memory, often with the accompanying positive or negative emotions associated with it. A large proportion of our thoughts will have similar triggers that we may be partly or entirely unconscious of – a bodily sensation such as nerves or excitement could trigger a thought about what we are worried about or looking forward to in the near future; something in our field of vision like a photo or object will trigger an associated thought attached to that object.

As humans we are always trying to make meaning of our experiences, and in this context – and in the context of our evolutionary history to be primed to be alert for danger and ensure survival – it makes sense that we give our inner thoughts a lot of weight. If we tend to be analytical or anxious, this can tip into something called rumination – a tendency to go over and over (and over!) the same negative thought loop, turning over the subject for every possible missed angle and often revisiting the same worry or detail many, many times. Rumination can be a seriously unpleasant experience, increasing anxious feelings, raising stress hormones, and taking us over the same ground without providing any helpful solutions.

We can use ACT techniques to notice these thoughts and rumination loops and decide whether or not to give them importance at any given moment. One of the most important questions in ACT techniques is 'is this thought helpful?' Note that the question **is NOT** 'is this thought true?' Whether a thought is true or not is often subjective, but it's much easier to tell whether or not it's helpful to us in relation to trying to meet our goals and our general sense of well-being in that moment.

For example, Max, an account manager in an advertising agency, came into coaching as he was struggling with procrastination around making client presentations, which often involved hard conversations on creative direction, tight budgets and high client expectations. During their first coaching session Louise asked Max to notice what thoughts, feelings and words arose in his mind when he put his attention on giving his next presentation to a notoriously tricky client.

> *'I'm a terrible speaker. I get so nervous people can see it. I hate every minute I'm up there'.*
>
> *'The client hates me and thinks I'm an idiot'.*
>
> *'I'm going to fail and get fired'.*
>
> *'I feel physically sick just thinking about it. I don't know if I can do it.'*

If someone close to Max was standing at his shoulder just before he was due to present, whispering in his ear *'You're a terrible speaker! Everyone can see what a nervous wreck you are! Everyone hates you! You're going to fail and get fired! You can't do it, and now you're going to throw up!'* what feelings would you guess he would be most likely to experience? Perhaps shame, panic, exposure, a sense of dread?

And how do you think this onslaught might affect his physical appearance and behaviour once he went up to make his presentation? Maybe a faltering voice, shaking hands, uncertain delivery, a strong desire (whether enacted or not) to run out of the room? I think it's fair to say that this little pep talk would be unlikely to help Max feel supported and confident in his ability to do a good job.

And yet, this is how many of us speak to ourselves much of the time when we need to do something we find difficult. At worst it's brutal. At best, it's entirely unhelpful.

So to unhook from these kinds of unhelpful thoughts, you can use this step-by-step technique which we have adapted from those described by Dr. Russ Harris in his book *The Happiness Trap*[8] and on his very helpful YouTube Channel.[9]

1) When you are thinking about doing (or about to do) something you find hard or are worried about, notice the thought or thoughts you are having or experiencing through your inner voice.

2) Just notice the words (or feelings or images if that's what comes up) and starting with the phrase: 'I am having the thought that...' put the thoughts into words – i.e. 'I am having the thought that this conversation is going to be a disaster.' You can simply think them to yourself, say them aloud or write them down. The important thing is to bring them into your conscious awareness.

3) Check out whether the thought has anything useful or informative to tell you. In the pursuit of self-awareness it's important we do reflect on our behaviour and gut instincts. So, in the case of 'I'm having the thought that the conversation is going to be a disaster' we could say that it's telling us the conversation is important to us and we are worried about it, and perhaps need to take some action.

4) Notice what is unhelpful about the thought. 'This conversation is going to be a disaster' is what we could call Catastrophic Thinking (this is one of the common Thinking Traps often referred to in Cognitive Behaviour Therapy – CBT). The thought is both extreme ('disaster!') and alarmingly definite ('it's going to happen!'). Unless we have the ability to see into the future, neither of these things is objectively true. And in any case the thought is *unhelpful* as it creates anxiety and lowers your optimism and confidence in your ability to handle it well.

5) Thank your mind. Yep, you read it right. Tell your mind 'Thanks mind, I know you are trying to help me but that thought is really unhelpful right now. I'm going to return to preparing for the conversation using the techniques

I've learned and make it a success,' or whatever form of words works for the unhelpful thought you are having, but always starting with acknowledging the thought and thanking your mind.

6) Get on with taking whatever positive, proactive action you need to, or focusing on something that aligns with your goals and values (e.g. focusing with full attention on a piece of work you need to do, spending time with your family). Each time the thought recurs, repeat step 5.

7) Replace the thought with something which is helpful, e.g. 'I know that I have the ability to handle the conversation well, and I believe in myself. Everything is ok.' Repeat as often as feels helpful, continuing to notice and unhook from any new unhelpful thoughts as they arise.

This may feel a little awkward to start with, and like any new habit can take a bit of practice to become comfortable. We invite you to commit to trying it for a few days to start with and see what happens. You will likely be surprised to notice the frequency of harsh thoughts you are having, and the number of negative messages you are telling yourself. Notice how good it feels to replace those with an alternative self-talk that feels supportive, helpful and reassuring. You can dial this up even more by adding a self-compassion practice, which we'll cover next.

Using self-compassion practices to regulate

At its heart, self-compassion is the practice of treating yourself with the same kindness, care and understanding that you would offer a close friend who is having a hard time with something. Rather than berating yourself for making mistakes or not being good enough in specific ways, self-compassion encourages you to approach these moments with a sense of gentleness, acceptance, even humour.

The idea of being kind to yourself being a good thing isn't new – related practices and philosophies have always been part of most major faiths, the most prominent being Buddhism. However, we think it's fair to say that most of us aren't very good at doing it. Self-compassion isn't just a 'nice-to-have' emotional skill – it turns out it's a profound and essential component of mental health and well-being. According to research by Kristen Neff and others, it reduces anxiety and depression, improves relationships, increases emotional resilience and motivation, and even promotes better physical health.[10]

In her ground-breaking research, Neff describes self-compassion as involving three main components:

Self-kindness vs Self-judgement: Self-compassion involves offering yourself warmth and understanding when you experience pain, rather than criticizing yourself for being imperfect.

Common humanity vs Isolation: Rather than feeling isolated or 'broken' when you face difficulties, self-compassion helps you see that everyone experiences setbacks and struggles. You are not alone in your pain.

Mindfulness vs Over-identification: Self-compassion encourages you to face your emotions with curiosity and kindness, noticing them without becoming overwhelmed or too involved in them.

How to cultivate self-compassion

Self-compassion is something we can do anytime, anywhere and for many people it can be a transformational step in their self-development – sometimes quite quickly.

Here are a few simple practices to get you started:

1) **Practice being kind to yourself as a first response**: When you experience failure or disappointment, treat yourself with kindness. Instead of saying to yourself something like, 'I'm such a failure,' try saying, 'It's ok to find things hard. I am learning and doing the best I can.'

2) **Use mindfulness to observe your emotions:** Allow yourself to feel your emotions without judgement. Practise mindfulness by focusing on your breath and noticing your feelings without trying to push them away or judge them. There are many guided self-compassion mindfulness meditations available for free online, as well as through the major well-being platforms such as Calm or Headspace.

3) **Write yourself a compassionate letter:** Imagine someone you love or care for is going through a tough time. What would you say to them? Write a letter to yourself, offering the same kindness, reassurance and understanding.

4) **Create compassionate self-talk:** Take some time to choose positive and reassuring phrases that resonate with you, such as, 'I am enough,' or 'I know I can do this,' and repeat them whenever you feel self-doubt or self-criticism arising.

Bottom-Up techniques

Breathing techniques

How many times have you heard the words 'just breathe' or 'take a deep breath' in moments of stress or panic? We instinctively know that our breath has the power to help us calm ourselves, but few of us know how to harness that power effectively. Breathing exercises work by tapping into the parasympathetic nervous system, the part of your body responsible for rest and digestion. When you engage in controlled, mindful breathing, such as slow, deep breaths, you stimulate the vagus nerve, which signals your body to calm down. This counteracts the body's fight-or-flight response, reducing your heart rate and lowering blood pressure, which in turn helps you feel more grounded and in control.

Research in 2023 by the neuroscientist Melis Balban, alongside her Stanford colleagues, has shown that incorporating breathwork into your daily routine can significantly reduce levels of cortisol (the stress hormone), promote emotional regulation and enhance cognitive function.[11] Whether it's a quick deep-breathing session during a stressful moment or regular practice to maintain a calm and balanced state, breathing exercises can transform your internal world and your external responses to conflict.

Getting started with breathing exercises

You don't need to spend hours practising to experience the benefits of controlled breathing. Below we'll share a few of the easiest evidence-based techniques we use in our coaching practice, starting with 'breathing by numbers'. There are many variations of this, all of which involve breathing in, holding the breath and breathing out for different numbers of seconds. There is some research that indicates a long, extended out breath is most effective in activating the parasympathetic nervous system and triggering physical relaxation and reducing stress. However, we've discovered that different patterns of breathing are effective for different people, so it's worth experimenting with a few to find the one that works best for you. In our own cases, Alice's go-to is Cadence Breathing (with a 3-3-6 count), whereas Louise prefers the longer 4-8-12 combination advised by Dr. Libby Weaver in her book *Rushing Woman's Syndrome*.[12] See what works for you.

How to use cadence breathing

Coordinating your breathing can take a little bit of getting used to, so the easiest place to start is with the shorter-length 3-3-6 in-hold-out combination. You can follow the same instructions and vary the combinations to see what works best for you.

Step 1: Get into position

> Find a comfortable position – sitting, standing or lying down. If possible, close your eyes to minimize distractions. Rest your hands on your lap or by your sides.

Step 2: Inhale for 3 seconds

Breathe in slowly and deeply through your nose, expanding your belly rather than just your chest. Imagine the breath filling your lower lungs.

Step 3: Hold for 3 seconds

Gently hold the breath. This brief pause helps stabilize oxygen levels and prevents shallow breathing patterns.

Step 4: Exhale for 6 seconds

Breathe out slowly and fully through your mouth. Exhaling longer than you inhale signals safety to your nervous system, encouraging relaxation. Imagine stress and tension leaving your body with each breath.

Step 5: Repeat for 2 to 10 minutes

Continue the cycle for at least five complete rounds, or longer if needed.

Some people can feel a little dizzy or hyperventilated when they start out with a breathing practice. If this happens to you, make sure you take a few minutes to breathe naturally and allow the feeling to pass before repeating the process if you still need to calm yourself further.

The physiological Sigh

You don't need to retreat to a quiet room for long periods of time to regain your composure. You can reset your nervous system in seconds, and one of the most effective techniques to do so is the Physiological Sigh – a simple but powerful tool championed by neuroscientist and Professor of Neurobiology, Andrew Huberman.[13] The beauty of the Physiological Sigh is that it's quick and unobtrusive, making it ideal for high-stress moments during your work day. It is ideal for use during or after a difficult conversation to get back to a state of calm, or before or after presentations if public speaking or presenting has a tendency to stress you out.

The Physiological Sigh is a natural, automatic response that the body uses to reduce stress. When you're sleeping, it often happens as part of the body's autonomic nervous system response – specifically, it helps the body expel excess carbon dioxide and regulate oxygen levels. While these sighs occur naturally, consciously employing the Physiological Sigh technique during the day can be a way to 'hack' this innate response. Huberman's research highlights the remarkable impact this technique has on the body's ability to reduce heart rate, lower blood pressure and counteract the body's fight-or-flight response. It is essentially a built-in tool for managing stress that you can leverage anytime, anywhere.

How to use the physiological sigh

Here's how to practise the Physiological Sigh when you feel stress mounting at work:

1) **Find a moment of stillness**: Even in a busy environment, try to find a moment of stillness. You don't need a private office to use this technique – simply take a brief pause in your work or during a conversation.

2) **Inhale deeply through your nose**: Begin by taking a deep, slow breath in through your nose, filling your lungs completely. Focus on expanding your diaphragm and allowing the breath to reach your lower lungs, not just your chest.

3) **Inhale again**: After your full inhale, take a second, shorter inhale, filling the top part of your lungs with more air. This extra inhale is key to fully expanding your lung capacity.

4) **Exhale slowly through your mouth**: Now, slowly exhale through your mouth, making the exhale longer than your inhalations. Ideally, your exhale should last **at least twice as long as the combined two inhales**. This prolonged exhalation is what sends the signal to your body to relax and activate the parasympathetic nervous system. Exhale until you feel your lungs are empty.

5) **Repeat:** You may need to repeat the process two or three times, depending on how tense you feel. With each cycle, you'll notice a greater sense of calm and focus settling in.

Everyday mindfulness

Mindfulness practices are often recommended as some of the best ways of increasing self-regulation and well-being, and the evidence base for their potential effects on both mental and physical health is impressive.[14] However, when we suggest creating a mindfulness habit to our leadership or conflict-coaching clients there is sometimes a look of unmistakable panic in their eyes. They just don't have *the time*. The good news is that we are not suggesting that anyone needs to sit in the lotus position for hours on end to get the benefits. The techniques we recommend don't require lots of practice or special settings – just a few minutes of your time and you're good to go.

Here we'll share two popular, effective, quick and easy mindfulness exercises you can try anytime.

The 5-4-3-2-1 mindful noticing technique

This is a simple but powerful grounding exercise that connects you with your senses and anchors you to the present. When anxiety, stress or overthinking takes over, this technique can quickly bring your focus back to the here and now.

How it works

- **5 things you can see:** Look around and name five things you can see. It might be the desk in front of you, a plant by the window or the pattern on the floor. The key is to focus your attention on your environment.
- **4 things you can touch:** Pay attention to what you can feel. This might be the texture of your clothing, the warmth of your coffee cup or the surface of a desk or chair. Engage your sense of touch to bring you back to your body.

- **3 things you can hear**: Tune into the sounds around you. You might hear the hum of traffic, birds chirping outside, or distant conversations. Focusing on sounds helps ground you in the moment.
- **2 things you can smell**: Take a moment to identify any scents around you. Maybe you can smell the fragrance of your soap, fresh air from an open window or even your lunch waiting. The sense of smell is often underutilized but can be powerful in reconnecting you with the present.
- **1 thing you can taste**: Lastly, notice what you can taste. It might be the lingering flavour of a recent meal, the freshness of your chewing gum or simply the taste of your own mouth.

The 'STOP' technique

A quick mindfulness method to ground yourself in less than a minute.

S – Stop: Pause what you're doing. Just for a moment, interrupt the autopilot.

T – Take a breath: Breathe in slowly and deeply. Let your attention rest on the breath – your anchor.

O – Observe: Notice what's happening.

- What sensations do you feel in your body?
- What thoughts are running through your mind?
- What emotions are present, without judgement?

P – Proceed: Continue with your task, now with more presence and awareness. Ask yourself: '*What's the next best step I can take?*'

See John Kabat-Zinn's *Wherever You Go, There You Are: Mindfulness Meditation in Everyday Life*, for more ideas to try.[15]

Exertion and exercise

As we explored earlier in this chapter, when stress or a sense of threat triggers the body's fight-or-flight response, adrenaline and cortisol levels rise, preparing the body for action. While this is useful in immediate danger, prolonged stress can cause these hormones to linger, leading to tension, anxiety and exhaustion. Physical exertion-based techniques can help process adrenaline efficiently, restoring balance to the nervous system.

While regular exercise is essential to overall physical and mental health, we all go through periods of our life during which regular exercise is either not possible or very difficult to fit in amongst all the other demands of our working, personal and family lives. In spite of this, we can still get some of the benefits of physical exertion for self-regulation in just a few minutes, without requiring any special clothing, equipment or training.

Below are two examples of exertion-based techniques which many of our clients find useful.

The tightening and release technique (or progressive muscle relaxation – PMR)

This method systematically engages and releases muscle groups to help discharge built-up tension and process excess adrenaline.

How to do it:

- Sit or lie down in a comfortable position. You can also do this standing if you can remain balanced and stable (again, safety first – be careful on that packed train!)
- Start at your feet. Tighten your foot muscles as hard as you can for 5 to 10 seconds, then release completely.
- Move upward through the body (legs, abdomen, chest, arms, shoulders, neck and face), tightening each muscle group for a few seconds before letting go.

- As you release, exhale slowly, visualizing stress leaving your body.
- Repeat for particularly tense areas.

High-intensity interval training (HIIT) for stress release

Short bursts of intense physical exertion followed by brief recovery periods help burn through excess adrenaline and boost endorphin production. During the Covid-19 pandemic all our coaching work switched to virtual video calls, and for periods of time many people (including us) were restricted on whether and how long they could leave the house, making many forms of exercise a challenge. The Covid lockdown era was an undeniably extremely stressful time for most of us, when many of our go-to stress-management strategies weren't accessible. Necessity being the mother of invention, to provide an alternative self-regulation strategy we introduced the idea of HIIT 'snacking' to our clients – taking a minute or two between calls (off camera) to do a series of jumping jacks, squats or burpees to burn off the stress from their previous conversation before starting the next.

This proved so effective that it's something we continue to recommend today. It's of course easier to do this if you work from home or have access to a private space such as your own office or an empty conference room. Even if you don't have the benefit of privacy, a fast walk or brief sprint around the block will do the same job. Get creative, and there's usually a way.

How to do it

Find a space where you can extend your arms and legs fully in all directions without striking anything, and where is private enough for you to feel comfortable. There are some workplaces where suddenly doing a minute of 'high knees' in the open plan office wouldn't raise an eyebrow, and others where this would be pretty distracting for everyone around you, so use your judgement. Remove any restrictive or warm top layers of clothing (like a jacket or sweater). If your shoes are inflexible or heeled, remove these too.

If you have any health concerns, especially heart or breathing problems or injuries, and are unsure if HIIT is suitable for you, please do seek medical advice before trying this technique.

1) Set a timer for either 30 or 60 seconds depending on your baseline fitness.
2) For the set time, engage in either: jumping jacks, squats, burpees or 'high knees' (running on the spot while raising your knees as high as you can).
3) Follow with 15 to 30 seconds of active recovery (walking or deep breathing).
4) Repeat another one to three times (depending on your stamina and the time available) varying the type of exercise.
5) Replace any removed clothes and shoes, and go back to your day.

If you can find time to do this once a day, over time you should experience an improvement in your overall stress levels. However, it can be used just-in-time, when you need to regulate or recover from feelings of accumulating stress in your body.

If you feel like you are going to lose it

If you know that you're not going to be able to stop yourself from blowing up or emotionally losing control in a way that you might regret – then take a deep breath and politely, calmly and respectfully exit the room (virtual or physical). A dramatic exit is never a good idea, however good it might feel to storm out and slam the door or abruptly end the call (this is just another form of acting out, and tends to simply escalate a situation). However, taking the decision to call a time-out and pick up the conversation at a time when you feel more able to have it calmly is to be applauded. Many of the unpleasant conflicts we have been called to de-escalate could have been avoided if someone had had the wisdom to just pause and let everyone calm down. We need more of those level heads in the world of work.

For more strategies on how to handle an unexpected turn for the worse in a hard conversation, go to the *Response* chapter.

Regulation summary

- **Self-regulation is the ability to manage your thoughts, emotions and behaviours under stress.**
- **It allows you to choose a deliberate response rather than react impulsively during conflict.**
- **The brain's stress responses – fight, flight, freeze and tend/befriend – shape how we behave under pressure and can be triggered by different conflict styles and personal stressors.**
- **Top-Down (mind-based) and Bottom-Up (body-based) techniques can help restore calm and control and what will work best for you is very individual.**
- **Practising regulation *before*, *during*, and *after* tough conversations helps you stay composed and effective.**

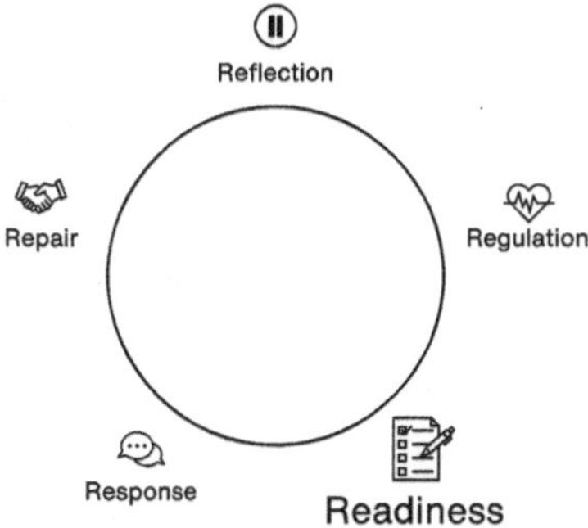

7

Readiness

'In preparing for battle, I have always found that plans are useless, but planning is indispensable.'
– Dwight D. Eisenhower[1]

This chapter will introduce you to everything you need to be as well prepared as possible, feeling ready to initiate almost any kind of hard conversation at work. *Readiness* is all about mapping out your plan A, and preparing you to successfully adapt to meet whatever happens in the moment (whether that's resorting to plan B… or plan Z). Thoughtfully preparing for hard conversations is a key tenet of Smart Conflict for two reasons. Firstly, because when we feel prepared, we increase our confidence and therefore our commitment to actually go and have the conversation. Without *Readiness* our anxiety and therefore our failure rate will be higher. Secondly, by preparing both our plan A, and a suite of other scenario-based strategic responses, we set ourselves up to successfully adapt as needed in the moment. This is a critical capability for hard conversations, given we cannot with certainty anticipate or control how other people will react. What we can do is plan our 'If X then Y' responses in advance.

There are two facets to *Readiness* that the tools and frameworks in this chapter cover: our way of 'being' in hard conversations, and our way of 'doing' them. The pioneering psychologist Carl Rogers emphasized an important distinction between 'being' and 'doing' in his work on personal growth and effective communication.[2] Our 'way of being' describes how we are, our mindset, presence and our energy. How we are experienced by others is largely informed by how they *feel* in our presence.[3] Our way of 'doing' can be understood as the actions we take and the tools, techniques and interventions we choose. Readiness requires us to carefully consider and consciously choose the way we show up, enabling us to create the conditions for Smart Conflict to thrive, and meaningful change to happen.

In this chapter we'll walk you through what to do to prepare fully for a hard conversation you plan to initiate, and the framework that will guide you through the conversation itself. We'll look at the being – what we can do to work on our mindset to create the conditions for Smart Conflict, before moving on to the highly practical 'doing' of our Hard Conversations Framework. For more on how to manage your response when you are *unexpectedly* on the receiving end of a hard conversation (one you couldn't have planned for) see the *Regulation* and *Response* chapters.

First things first: Does it need saying?

And does it need saying by you? Before we dive into the details on how to be and what to do to increase your chances of succeeding in your next hard conversation, we want you to carefully consider if the conversation needs to happen at all. Not every single issue that arises needs to be addressed directly or immediately, particularly if it's clear that having the conversation won't achieve anything productive, or even positive. There are some situations where you should actively choose *avoidance* as a conflict style (what we call *strategic avoidance*) rather than open up a hard conversation that won't get you – or anyone – anywhere useful.

Here are some reasons you might choose not to have a hard conversation at work:

1) If the colleague is leaving the team or organization soon, you might decide investing further in this working relationship is not a priority or a good use of your time.
2) If emotions are heightened for either or both of you, you might choose to wait until the initial intensity has died down to have the conversation when you are both more regulated, and have a little distance from the triggering event.
3) You are aware of or are concerned that your colleague might have some mental health or personal challenges that might make this a bad time to open a hard conversation, and/or make them less able to cope or respond resourcefully.
4) If the incident is a one-off and the impact not serious (and raising it may give more importance than it warrants right now).
5) If the issue is not impacting you or the work, solving it is objectively not your responsibility, and getting involved could be perceived as interfering (although be honest with yourself on this one – this is a common excuse for avoidance!)
6) If there is nothing the other person can realistically do in response to your raising it (circumstances out of their control).
7) If your HR guidelines instruct you to follow a specific process around certain types of hard conversations (e.g. regarding misconduct or serious performance problems) and you must be guided by that.
8) If the outcome and impact of the conversation is likely to result in reduced morale and motivation at a time where morale is already low, you might choose to prioritize more positive and optimistic messages. For example, raising a small issue that is not having a serious impact could do more harm than good and not be in the best interests of

the group at that moment (this is a time to consider 'not sweating the small stuff').

9) If you are not the right person to have it, i.e. you do not have the authority or permission, or based on your current relationship with the other person there is a good chance that your involvement will make things worse (in the latter case, the task is to find the right person to have the conversation rather than simply ignore it).

10) You don't have all the information you need to have the conversation productively (in which case – get it).

The Smart Conflict decision tree: Should I have this hard conversation?

So, should you have that conversation or not? We've designed this decision tree shown in Figure 5 to help you decide if this is a hard conversation you should have right now, or if it's one you would be better off strategically delaying, delegating or avoiding altogether. If the decision tree has led you to conclude that yes, now is the right time for the conversation and you are the person to have it, there are two questions we want you to really reflect on before you press on:

1) What am I trying to achieve by having this conversation?

2) Is my goal in having this conversation in service of something beyond myself and my own personal dissatisfaction?

If your answer to the first question ('*What am I trying to achieve by having this conversation?*') is anything that sounds like '*I want them to know how annoyed I am about it*' and you don't have a goal in mind beyond expressing dissatisfaction, then we'd gently encourage you to think about identifying a goal for the conversation that allows you to answer *yes* to question 2 ('*Is my goal in having this conversation in service of something beyond myself and my own personal dissatisfaction?*'). A self-orientated goal might

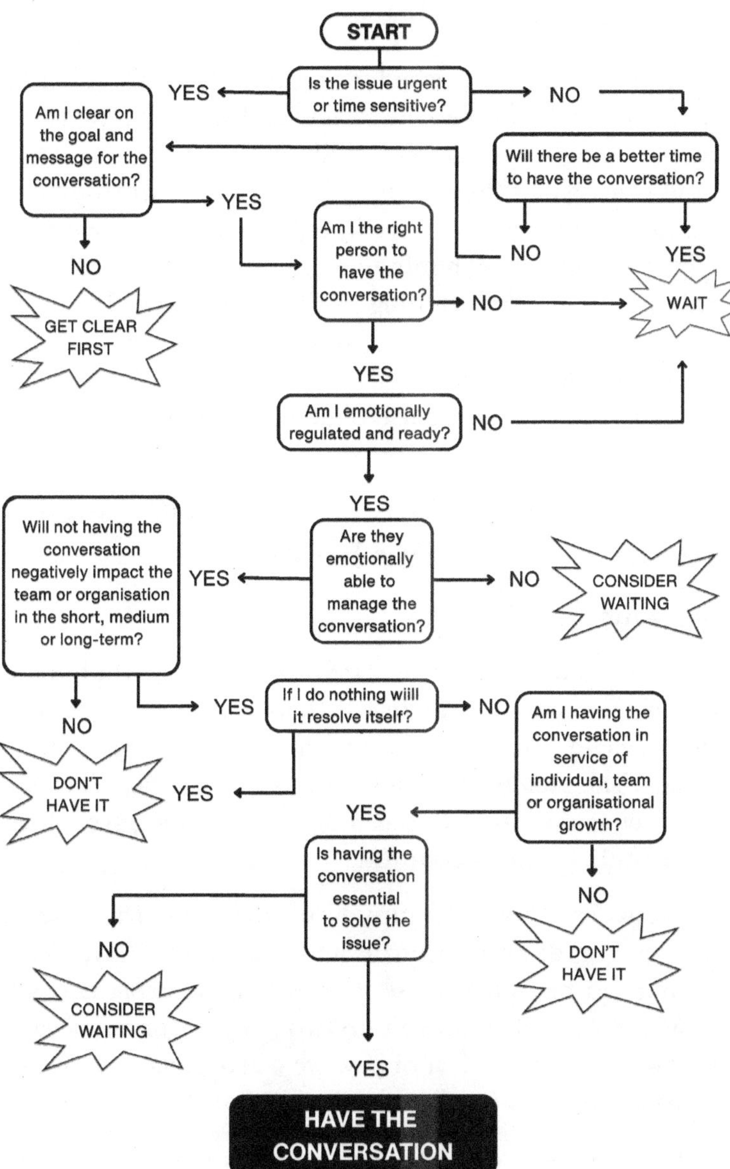

Figure 5: The Hard Conversation decision tree
Source: Driscoll & van Haarst, 2025

sound like: *'I want you to know I don't like how fast you talk'.* An in-service goal might sound like: *'I want to talk about how we can improve our communication together, because I struggle to keep up with your fast pace sometimes'.*

If at this point you feel satisfied it's right to move ahead, the rest of this chapter will outline how to get you from deciding to do it, to actually doing it, and doing it well. Just because we've decided we should have a hard conversation doesn't always provide enough motivation to go ahead and do it, especially if our own fearful thoughts and feelings are reminding us of all the potential dangers of getting it wrong, and warning us not to go ahead. This will be more of a challenge for you if you know you tend to adopt *Avoidant* or *Accommodating* conflict styles (head back to the *Reflection* chapter if you need a refresher on your Default Conflict Styles).

The 'being' of readiness – mindsets and tools for overcoming blocks

Facing your fears head on

For those of you who recognize that a fear of conflict is holding you back from having some or all the hard conversations you know you should be having, *Readiness* requires a direct confrontation with those fears. The exercise we will walk you through here shows you exactly how to do just that. But first, here is some psychological context to help us unpick our fears.

When we worry about a future event, the anticipatory anxiety we feel can be disproportionate and misleading – the fear of something can be much worse than our actual experience of it. This fear can be broken down into two key categories: a fear of a negative outcome, and a fear of how we will *respond emotionally* to a negative outcome. We might fear one or both of these.

At its extreme, our fears of negative outcomes can spiral into exaggerated and irrational thinking, known as catastrophizing. In this cognitive distortion we predict the worst possible outcome, believing it's far more likely than it actually is. For example, you might worry that receiving negative feedback on a presentation will result in you losing your job, or that if you show any sign of dissatisfaction with a team member, the relationship will completely, and unrecoverably, break down.

In addition to being bad at judging realistic outcomes, research in 2000 and 2003 by Daniel Gilbert and Timothy Wilson has shown that we frequently misjudge our own emotional reactions to future events[4] (known as 'impact bias'), and that we tend to amplify and overestimate the negative impact of future adverse events, mispredicting both their intensity and duration (known as 'affective forecasting error').[5] For example, you might feel like you'll be '*devastated for weeks*' after receiving some unwelcome developmental feedback, or you'll '*never get over the embarrassment*', but in reality, you process your emotions effectively in a few days, and are back on track before you know it.

It's no wonder then, with this kind of distorted negative thinking (and all the horrible feelings it triggers) that we aren't very motivated to go and have the hard conversation we know we should. Pair this with the human survival mechanism of *negativity bias* – the psychological tendency to focus more on negative past experiences than positive ones[6] (see the *Regulation* chapter for more on how to overcome this) and we can find ourselves petrified by the stories we are telling ourselves about what could go wrong. If you do find yourself ruminating about your worst fears, it might help to focus on the fact that not only are our worst fears unlikely to come true, but the balance of probability is that whatever happens it won't feel as bad as you think it will. And even when really difficult things do happen, we tend to be much more resilient than we think we are in navigating our way through them.

The anxiety audit

Very often, the solution to anxiety is action. Just knowing it probably won't be that bad might be helpful, but going a step further and creating scenario-based plans for a number of possible eventualities will help you mitigate risks, and get into problem-solving mode. Research by Camellia Torabizadeh and her colleagues in 2018[7] and Gergö Hadlaczky and colleagues in 2024[8] suggests that when we consciously switch into problem-solving mode and identify specific actions to address our real or perceived problems, our anxiety reduces and our confidence in our ability to cope with the future increases.

This 15-minute exercise, informed by Cognitive Behavioural Therapy (CBT) approaches, invites you to converse directly with your fears and get into problem-solving mode as an anxiety reducing strategy:

Ask yourself these questions in turn:

1) How afraid do I feel about having the hard conversation right now from 0 to 10 – 0 being no anxiety at all, and 10 being I am experiencing significant physical sensations or effects of anxiety (e.g. raised heart rate, rapid breathing, lightheadedness, stomach upset, insomnia)?
2) When I think about having the conversation, what exactly is my fear?
3) What is the worst-case scenario I can think of?
4) What if anything can I do to mitigate this happening?
5) If the worst does happen, what's my best plan of action? And if that didn't work, what would be plan B?
6) How afraid do I feel now about having the hard conversation, from 0 to 10?
7) Did my score change at all?
8) What would I need to know or do to reduce my anxiety by one more number along the scale?

Review your answers. Then, try and take a mental step back and ask yourself if they are a realistic assessment, or are you still being too negative? If so, ask yourself what you could do differently. What would you do if you felt no fear at all? Is it possible you could experiment with an element of this in a safe way to test this strategy? Are there any clues there as to how you could reduce your anxiety by another point or two? If so, go back and update your 'best plan' with these ideas. How does that change your score from 0 to 10 now?

Feel the fear... and do it anyway

Exposure is widely integrated into CBT frameworks, and is used particularly successfully in the treatment of anxiety disorders, PTSD, and phobias. It can play a useful role for those of you for whom having a hard conversation triggers a level of anxiety that leads to avoidance of the conversation altogether. As the name might suggest, Exposure asks us as per the title of Susan Jeffers' famous book to '*feel the fear and do it anyway*'.[9] Among many other similar studies, a research review in 2012 by Mohammed Milad and his colleagues showed that when we repeatedly expose ourselves to the situations we fear, our anticipatory anxiety diminishes.[10] This exposure retrains the brain's threat response system and, over time, the amygdala (the brain's fear centre that we learned about in the *Regulate* chapter) learns that the previously feared stimulus is not as dangerous as it once believed.

Cognitive behavioural therapists suggest starting small (known as graded exposure), rather than jumping into the deep end and a scenario that is the most scary in our mind. The aim is not to throw you into your panic zone, but to build up your tolerance over time and increase the level of risk you feel you are taking, step by step. We use a similar approach in our coaching work – we would always encourage clients to start with small, safe experiments when facing their fear of hard conversations, starting with something low risk. So, for example, telling your slightly grumpy colleague you can't make their preferred meeting slot for a low-importance check-in (saying yes meaning you would have to rearrange your whole calendar on an already packed day) and can only do a specific time slot. Saying a polite but firm no, when you would usually reluctantly say yes to avoid the fear of causing bad feelings. Once you see that nothing bad happens, you can keep practising reinforcing this kind of boundary around your time until it becomes completely comfortable. Then move on to your next experiment.

So to get you started, what small, relatively low risk hard conversation could you have this week?

As we close this section on facing your fears, we'd encourage you to remember, when all hell breaks loose (or you just worry that it will!) almost everything is *figureoutable*. There's usually a way through and beyond even the trickiest of situations. In time and with a bit of preparation you'll soon be looking back and thinking, 'yes that was hard, but I got through it, and it wasn't as bad as I thought!'

Redefining kind

When we ask people what gets in the way of them having hard conversations, one of the most common reasons we are given is that they fear being unkind to the other person. This is usually a combination of worries about the act of saying something uncomfortable, difficult or potentially critical (the content), and about choosing the wrong words (the delivery). Being worried about hurting someone's feelings is admirable, and a clear indication of empathy – considering the emotions of others, and our impact on them. When we ask our masterclass participants to define *kindness* and *care* they typically respond with words like 'thoughtful,' 'empathetic' and 'respectful.' Sometimes (but less often) someone also offers up 'honesty.' In our view, these words form a key part of what it is to be kind. But they don't tell the whole story.

Here's our definition of kindness at The Power House:

> *'The practice of acting with respect, honesty and compassion whilst prioritizing the growth and well-being of others'*

For us, the *whole* story of kindness requires the inclusion of the latter part of this definition '*whilst prioritizing the growth and well-being of others*'. Because as we explored in the *Reflection* chapter, feeling we are growing and progressing as an individual in the world is a core human need. None of us wants the year ahead to be an exact re-run of the year that's just been, or to feel that we are doing the same things, the same way, with the same results, day in and day out. Without momentum, evidence of new learning and incremental improvement, our well-being suffers and we can feel we're stagnating and stuck. So it follows that the kindest thing we can do for our colleagues and our teams is our very best to enable their growth. And how do we do that? By giving clear, specific, genuine feedback and sharing hard truths in conversations which bring high support and high challenge in equal measure. You can use our Five-Step Hard Conversations Framework (explained in detail later in this chapter) to do so.

The right kind of confidence

Not all confidence is created equal when it comes to Smart Conflict. In fact there is a very specific confidence that serves us in constructive conflict, and another form that will just get in our way.

In his 2021 book, *Think Again*, Adam Grant shares the optimal mindset for influencing others to rethink their fixed positions. He calls it 'confident humility', which he defines as when we have '*faith in our capability, while appreciating that we may not have the right solution or even be addressing the right problem*'. Grant encourages us to '*admit that we're a work in progress [and] show that we care more about improving ourselves than proving ourselves.*'[11] Bullish self-confidence without humility results in what Grant calls 'blind arrogance'; and where an abundance of humility dominates without the necessary confidence, 'debilitating doubt' follows.

At the heart of the confident humility mindset is an understanding of our own limitations, particularly our limited ability to see every angle and know the right decision in any given situation. This is nicely illustrated by the *Dunning-Kruger Effect*, first identified by psychologists David Dunning and Justin Kruger in 1999.[12] This cognitive bias explains how people with low competence in a particular area tend to overestimate their abilities (known as 'the peak of mount stupid'), while those with high competence are more likely to doubt themselves. In short, the less we know, the more confident we feel – and the more we know, the more we realize how much we *don't* know.

So if we can recognize that we all have blind spots, and understand that an overconfidence in our ideas is an expression of the need to be right (Inflexible) rather than to get it right (Collaborative) we can approach conversations and debates with others with a new goal – not to persuade, but to use curiosity to actively seek out different perspectives, and be open to changing our own minds depending on what we discover along the way.

Support and challenge

Often when we arrive to work with an organization where there isn't enough Smart Conflict, or where performance feedback is woolly and hard conversations aren't happening (these factors usually go together), people expect us to turn up and say, '*Right, that's enough of being kind and supportive! You all need to put on your big pants and start being a lot tougher!*' And this is understandable, as most people tend to think of hard conversations as being a choice between using either carrot or stick. They are then relieved to discover that isn't our approach, and that there is a much more effective way.

Sanford's Support and Challenge model, first developed in the 1960s, is based on his research that found a combination of an equal measure of high support *and* high challenge is optimum for individual, team and organizational growth.[13] It's a key 'way of being' for Smart Conflict because it's only when our people feel they are getting both that they can thrive and grow. The model presents the four combinations which can inform the communication culture, and we describe below the typical results we see as a consequence of each.

High support + Low challenge = Comfort

When we are led with this balance we experience Comfort. In this context, comfort can be understood as being in implementation mode. It's sometimes described as 'stagnation', and whilst in cultures where this is present there are usually strong working relationships, there is likely to be a lack of development or learning. For this reason we talk about Comfort being pretty uncomfortable, leading to frustration and inertia.

High challenge + Low support = Anxiety

This combination leads us to feeling anxious and stressed. In an organization or a relationship that is low on support you might find a cultural fear of speaking up, a lack of idea sharing, tension, blame and low trust between colleagues.

Low support + Low challenge = Apathy

When we have low support and low challenge, we are without leadership of any kind, and this vacuum breeds apathy. Here we lack motivation and drive to take action, feel disconnected and disinterested, and find it difficult to create new ideas.

High Support + High Challenge = Growth

High Support *and* High Challenge underpin Smart Conflict, because a good supply of both sets up an environment for growth. In this space we might feel a strong connection with our colleagues, be willing to take the risk of getting into healthy challenge and constructive conflict with our teammates, and as an organization will see high levels of innovation and resilience to change. Cultures high in both support and challenge share ideas freely, feel safe to make mistakes, and give and receive open and regular feedback.

After taking thousands of leaders and managers through our Smart Conflict training we've come to the conclusion that most people think they must make a binary choice between offering people only high support or high challenge, i.e. a choice between creating Comfort or Anxiety. The quotient of support and challenge can be offered in the context of one hard conversation, over the course of a day, or over a week. What's key is that within the relationship, your colleague (or your team) feels they have a good balance of both from you in the round.

One simple way of finding out the answer to this question is simply to ask your team how supported and challenged they feel by you today. By increasing your (and your team's) self-awareness around how supported and challenged everyone is feeling *today*, you might uncover that different people are experiencing your leadership or the organization differently, and that their needs, appetite and tolerance for challenge might be very different.

Support and challenge in action

Here are some examples of how you could create an environment where people feel both supported and valued, but not overly stretched and anxious.

Setting clear expectations and stretch goals with support and challenge

If we're setting ambitious targets, we need to acknowledge these won't be easy to achieve, communicate our belief in their ability to achieve hard things, and finally offer our coaching and support to set them up for success.

That might sound like: '*I know this is a stretch goal, but I believe in your ability to make it happen. Let's set up weekly check-ins to tackle any roadblocks together.*'

Encouraging constructive conflict and diverse perspectives

In a team meeting, when two team members disagree we can see our role as helping to facilitate a valuable debate. We can do this by identifying that there are divergent perspectives, signalling that all views are welcome, refocus discussion from 'who is right' to 'what is right' and always come back to the problem that needs solving.

That might sound like: '*How interesting that you both have such strong and different views. Taking a step back, thinking about the shared goal, with all the data and perspectives, what are the best ideas we should be debating?*'

Delegating responsibility with trust and accountability

To move away from micromanaging (painful for you both and certainly not the way to extract the maximum value from whoever is on the receiving end), we need to give clear ownership and decision permissions, clarify roles and show confidence and support.

That might sound like: '*I trust you to lead this and make key decisions. I'm here as an advisor if you need me, but I want you to take full ownership of the outcome.*'

Calling out mediocrity without derailing motivation

If a team member is under-delivering it's important not to sugar-coat the truth, and to offer challenge, not simply criticism. You can do this by challenging them to raise the bar moving forward and focusing on the impact of the underperformance (focus on what good looks like in the future, spend as little time as possible criticizing past performance) and finally showing support.

That might sound like this: '*We can both agree there have been too many mistakes in your reports this quarter. The client is losing confidence in our reporting accuracy, which is putting us at risk of losing them to a competitor. I have high confidence in your ability to solve this, and re-build their trust. I'm here to help you in any way you need.*'

Doing it well – the key skills for hard conversations

So far in this chapter we've looked at how we can decide if we should have the conversation, and once we have decided we should, how we can get into the best possible mindset to make sure we have it, and have it well. Now we're turning our attention to look at the things we need to 'do' in order to be ready for a hard conversation, and the tools and frameworks you can use to develop them.

Skill 1: Getting clear on your message

> *'The single biggest problem in communication is the illusion that it has taken place.' – George Bernard Shaw*[14]

We are constantly reminded when we train teams and peer groups in our Smart Conflict methodology that it's often the simplest things that have the most impact. The importance of getting clear on your message is one of those things. Preparing for a hard conversation ahead of time is something that can be the work of minutes but have a seismic impact on the conversation's outcome. And although it might sound glaringly obvious in theory, in practice most of us don't prepare much – if at all – arriving into a meeting without giving it a moment's thought (perhaps we hadn't even clocked it in our diary) and hoping for the best. And suddenly, here we are faced with the eager and anxious face of the dependable team member hoping for good news about their long awaited promotion; or with the stony expression of the new project lead unhappy about their performance feedback; or the inscrutable visage of the boss who has called you in for a 'chat about how last week's pitch went'. With no advance preparation we can find ourselves scrabbling around trying to work out what kind of conversational ground we've landed on and what words to say, especially when we are giving (or receiving) news that is unexpected and not what was hoped for.

Scrabbling around for words in a panic does not usually result in clear and kind communication. It doesn't translate to others as professional and poised. And turning up and hoping for the best is rarely a strategy that will get the outcome you want from a hard conversation. There are of course some people who are prodigiously skilled at spontaneous communication, but for the rest of us, the best we can usually hope for is to come out of it having expressed our general intentions, and without having done any real damage. The worst – and this is something we see often as conflict coaches – is that we will misspeak, blurt out something we don't mean, over-promise, overreact, become tongue-tied or emotional, come across as too anxious, too angry, too dismissive. In other words, we make an absolute mess of it, which then takes time and effort to fix (if we can fix it at all).

So the first job of *Readiness* is to get clear on the message you want to land with the receiver ahead of time.

How do I get clear on my message?

Ask yourself: *What* exactly *do I want them to leave the conversation hearing and understanding with absolute clarity?*

Then write it down, or put it in a note in your phone. A few bullet points will usually be enough. Think about the specific words you want to use (and the ones you want to avoid). Read it over: is it clear, or a bit too woolly and indirect? Is it a bit too blunt, and would benefit from more of a gentle start up? Test the words in your mouth – how does it feel to say them? Is there anything you need to add, or take away?

Let's look at some examples now of what a clear message might sound like in a few different contexts:

A feedback message

'I want them to hear that this morning's presentation was not well received by the CEO because it was too long to hold her attention and did not contain the right data for her to feel informed'

A request for action

'I want them to hear that I need them to take on some additional workload while a colleague is away on extended leave'

A critical piece of information

'I want them to hear that the role they are currently doing is being largely replaced with AI and their role will be evolving significantly as a result'

A bid for repair

'I want them to know the conversation we had yesterday was upsetting for me, and I want them to see that it matters to me how they feel about what happened too and that we work together to identify how we might get things back on track'

For more on how to repair relations after a rupture with someone (or a group of people) see the *Repair* chapter.

By having this clarity ahead of time you are more likely to say what you mean, and they in turn are much more likely to hear what was intended. It will also provide you with a north star to help keep you on track as the conversation progresses in case it goes in an unintended, unexpected and/or unhelpful direction. Have your bullet points on hand in a notebook if you need a reminder or want to check you are on message as you go.

There are two things you should get clear about before a hard conversation:

1) What you need the other person to understand.
2) What you want them to do as a result of this message (it might be nothing).

Once you are clear on what you want to land, you can use our Five-Step Hard Conversations Framework (Figure 5) to give you a clear structure to navigate, from delivering a clear message, to exploring next steps and agreeing on any actions you both need to take.

Readiness doesn't only apply to when you need to deliver a message. Remember that it's equally important to be ready when you are going into a conversation when you're not sure what you're going to hear, or where your main job is to listen and respond to feedback. Being prepared can make a huge difference to how the conversation goes, and what happens next. You can scenario plan in advance using the Five-Step Hard Conversations Framework. See the *Response* chapter for more tools and techniques for when you are on the receiving end of hard conversations.

Skill 2: Structuring the conversation for success

The Five-Step Hard Conversations Framework

We have developed this framework as a step-by-step guide for how you can initiate almost any kind of hard conversation and increase your chances of achieving the response and engagement you are looking for from others.

Our Five-Step Hard Conversations Framework, shown in Figure 6, draws on everything we know about what drives success for our clients, and is built on the evidence base and proven elements of many models and techniques that have gone before, including but not limited to the Situation-Behavior-Impact (SBI) framework devised by the Center for Creative Leadership[15] and Marshall Goldsmith's *FeedForward* technique (see his book *What Got You Here Won't Get You There* or his YouTube videos for practical examples).[16]

What this Framework will not do is make all hard conversations feel easy. Some really might. But some will still feel hard – for you, and/or others. The framework should support you in feeling that the hard work and tricky feelings are at least worth it, because the conversation achieved something positive, in the direction of growth, for the task *and* the relationship.

The Framework contains five steps: Permission, Observation, Impact, Curiosity and Action, a quick reference guide to each step and a prompt on what you could say to open the conversation at each step.

		SAY...
PERMISSION	• SHARE CONTROL	• WOULD YOU LIKE FEEDBACK ON 'X' • WHEN WOULD BE A GOOD TIME TO TALK ABOUT 'X'
OBSERVATION	• WHAT'S THE SITUATION? • WHAT SPECIFIC BEHAVIOUR OR OUTCOME NEEDS HIGHLIGHTING?	• I NOTICED THAT... • I'VE BEEN MADE AWARE THAT...
IMPACT	• HIGHLIGHT THE IMPACT OF THE OUTCOME OR BEHAVIOR ON YOU/THE TEAM/THE ORGANIZATION.	• THE RESULT OF WHICH IS... • WHAT THAT HAS LED TO IS...
CURIOSITY	• ASK THEM WHAT THEY HAVE UNDERSTOOD • ASK FOR THEIR PERSPECTIVE ON THE ISSUE & IDEAS FOR SOLUTIONS • ASK HOW NOT WHY, SUSPEND JUDGEMENT. • SUMMARIZE THEIR THOUGHTS AND ACKNOWLEDGE EMOTIONS	• COULD YOU SUMMARIZE WHAT YOU'VE UNDERSTOOD FROM ME SO FAR? • WHAT'S YOUR UNDERSTANDING OF THE SITUATION? • WHAT DO YOU THINK SHOULD HAPPEN NEXT?
ACTION	• COLLABORATE TO GENERATE SOLUTIONS & NEXT STEPS • SEE IF THEY CAN OWN ACTIONS & COMMITMENTS • WHEN WILL YOU REVIEW AGAIN? • REPAIR AS NEEDED	• LET'S REVIEW ON 'X' DATE TO TRACK PROGRESS • I CAN SEE THIS HAS BEEN A HARD CONVERSATION. IS THERE ANYTHING ELSE YOU NEED FROM ME RIGHT NOW?

Figure 6: Five-Step Hard Conversations Framework
Source: Driscoll & van Haarst, 2025

While it's straightforward and largely intuitive to follow, there's a bit of theory and context it's useful to understand to give you the best chance of success. Here is a breakdown of each step in turn, and the key tools and mindsets you need to deliver each step effectively.

Step 1: Permission

Feeling a sense of autonomy and control is a fundamental human need.[17] When we receive unsolicited feedback or unwelcome news unexpectedly, or are surprised by an event we perceive as negative, we feel ambushed and out of control, triggering our threat response and resulting in resistant, defensive or aggressive behaviours.

But there's a simple thing you can do right upfront to bypass this, that gives the receiver what they need psychologically to feel they are in control behind the wheel (at least partially). And that simple thing is to ask for permission. There is a direct correlation between how in control someone feels, and how productive and emotionally regulated the conversation is going to be.

When we ask permission before initiating a difficult conversation we are priming the recipient for the conversation before it officially starts, and signalling that we are not assuming power and control. By inviting them gracefully into an adult-to-adult dialogue rather than acting like a bossy parent or a frustrated or frightened child, we set the tone for more receptive, thoughtful and measured engagement. Even when a conversation is compulsory and unavoidable – e.g. a formal performance review or appraisal – we can introduce elements of permission and control in how we invite the other person to join us.

In our experience it's unlikely someone will say 'no' if we open with 'would you be open to a conversation about…' but the consideration it confers can create a lot of goodwill. If they *do* say no, it's perhaps a sign that they or the relationship isn't in a robust enough place, and it might not be the right moment – which is still good information to have. If someone does refuse your invitation, it can be an opportunity to explore the underlying reasons for their resistance to a discussion and you might follow up with an open question like: 'I hear that you'd rather not talk about this right now; could you help me understand why?' While it's important to tread carefully if the answer is defensive or emotionally charged (there have been occasions where clients have told us team members have answered '*because I don't trust it won't be used against me*' or '*because I am not interested in criticism from management*') understanding where they are coming from will allow you to plan what you might need to change about your approach to the conversation (or the organizational feedback culture at large), rather than simply accepting it won't happen.

There are a number of ways you can introduce an element of permission to a hard conversation depending on the context you are in:

- Creating a sense of control around *if* they are willing to have the conversation.
- Offering choice and control about *when* the conversation takes place.
- Offering flexibility on *where* and in what format the conversation takes place to make them most comfortable and receptive.

In Table 2, we offer some phrases our clients have used to successfully create a sense of permission, alongside some pros and cons to be aware of.

A note on 'where' to have a hard conversation

We've often heard that it's received wisdom that the honourable thing to do is to have difficult conversations face to face, in person. That anything else is considered disrespectful in some way. Putting respect, kindness and care as a high priority in hard conversations is something we want to encourage, but we have also heard from many people we've coached (and there is a growing data set to

Table 2: Permissions table

Permission type	Phrase	Pros	Cons
If	'I had some ideas about [x]. Is that something you are looking for feedback on?' 'I've observed something I think is impacting [x]. Can we have a discussion about it?' 'I think it's important that we clear the air on [x]. I'd appreciate your willingness to talk it through. Would you be open to that?'	Great for: Managing up, especially if you are not clear about whether you have the 'authority' to give feedback or open a hard conversation. You would like to give some 'in the moment' feedback, but aren't sure how it will be received. You've had a difficult exchange with someone and you aren't sure where they are emotionally.	Not helpful: If you definitely plan to give the feedback, or it's time sensitive and you would not take 'no' or 'not now' for an answer.
When	'When would be a good time to talk about [x[?' 'Would you prefer to discuss it now, or on Monday?'	Times when you plan to give the feedback or have the conversation, but you are flexible on when it happens.	Not good for urgent feedback. If feedback is delayed it can be less impactful.

(Continued)

Table 2: (Continued)

Permission type	Phrase	Pros	Cons
Where	'Would you prefer to have the meeting on zoom or in person?' 'Would you like to go for a walk or stay in the office to talk it through?'	Times when you can't give autonomy over 'if' or 'when.'	The need to share feedback urgently might limit the location options.

support this idea), that for some, another setting, such as a phone or video call, can feel less confrontational and intense, and provide a 'safer' way to receive difficult news.[18]

When it comes to 'where,' our personal preferences around this will differ significantly, so we encourage you to be led by the recipient on where the difficult conversation takes place whenever possible, because the more comfortable they feel, and the more they feel they had a say in the matter, the better the conversation is going to go.

By granting them autonomy in just one of these areas – *if*, *when* or *where* – you will make the conversation feel like something that is being done *with* the person rather than *to* them and significantly increase the chances of a constructive outcome.

Step 2: Make observations

> *'It sounds ridiculous, but the shift to making observations about things I have actually seen and heard has changed everything. I never knew how to form the words. This has unblocked me.'*
>
> Anna, Masterclass Participant in Audit

One of the reasons hard conversations can go so wrong is that we charge in with opinions and assumptions, and make the fatal error of mistaking our feelings for facts. When we enter a conversation with our minds already made up, it's no surprise that we don't inspire other people to open theirs. It's hard to want to converse when we feel spoken *to* (or worse spoken *at*) not spoken *with*.

To keep the dialogue constructive, it's essential to make observations, not judgements. Often, we don't even realize just how much judgement creeps into our everyday language, but to be skilled at Smart Conflict it's essential to suspend it. The difficult bit is that this requires us to recognize we are being judgemental in the first place, and to be much more conscious and considered about the words we choose to express our thoughts and feelings about the behaviour and actions of others.

To be clear, it's not possible to remain non-judgemental at all times, however much some people protest they are. Being judgemental is deeply rooted in human evolution and serves as a survival mechanism to categorize and evaluate information swiftly and often subconsciously (we could also call it 'having good judgement'). There is substantial empirical research concluding that attempting to suppress or deny undesirable thoughts can actually lead to increased physiological stress.[19] So while it's impossible and not even desirable to banish all the judgey things we might think about someone else, it's important to focus on the facts.

Observations aim to be objective, and draw on evidence, not opinion. They describe what was seen, heard or experienced, avoiding interpretations or assumptions. Judgements, by contrast, introduce blame and emotion. By focusing on observations, you create a neutral, fact-based foundation that encourages engagement without triggering defensiveness, one of the most common pathways to shame, and a key ingredient of Destructive Conflict.

Non-violent communication: Speaking from 'I'

A game-changing technique drawn from Marshall Rosenberg's very useful 2003 book *Nonviolent Communication* is what he calls 'speaking from "I"'.[20]

'I' statements help keep our language neutral and grounded in our own experience and view of the world. Starting statements with 'you' often sounds accusatory and aggressive, provoking a defensive response from others. Nobody likes to be told who they are, or what they are thinking or feeling, and even if our assumptions are correct, presenting an assumption as a fact usually results in resistance.

'I' statements allow you to express your thoughts and feelings while inviting curiosity and openness and sound like this:

> '*What I observe is…*'
>
> '*What I've noticed is…*'
>
> '*I feel that…*'
>
> '*I need…*'
>
> '*What I think is…*'
>
> '*I would like…*'
>
> '*I'm concerned that…*'
>
> '*I have been made aware that…*'

But speaking from 'I' alone is not enough to prevent us from sounding judgemental. '*I think you are lazy*' is an 'I' statement that is very judgey indeed, and not a factual observation. An observation would be '*I have noticed that you were over an hour late every day this week. I feel frustrated that you haven't kept your commitment to be on time for work*'.

Think about the message you want to deliver in your next hard conversation. Using 'I' statements, how can you make factual observations about the situation, behaviour or task you want to talk about?

Step 3: Impact

Once we've created a sense of permission and made our non-judgemental observation, to increase the chances of instigating a behaviour change in others we now need to share the impact of the behaviour or action on the situation at hand.

It's well-established in the field of psychology that to change behaviour we need three things to be true: we need to want to change, we need to know how to change, and we need to be committed to doing it now (see the *Making it stick* chapter for more on creating and sustaining behaviour change).

By outlining clearly what the impact of what we've observed has been, we can unlock the other person's understanding of why a change is important, and increase their motivation to make a change as a result.

Here's an example of how an observation followed by an impact statement might sound:

> '*I noticed you interrupted me three times in today's meeting*' (observation), '*so I gave up trying to share the data. I'm worried that you are not in a position to make an informed decision*' (impact).

You can use some of the sentence starters in Table 3 to prepare your Observation and Impact statements. Notice that in these statements we are aiming to be as specific as possible about the impact using clear, professional but descriptive language. Remember, clear is kind.

Step 4: Curiosity

So, if you've followed the steps so far, you would have clearly set out your stall for the conversation you need to have. Now is the time to demonstrate your curiosity about what's going on for the other person: what they think and feel about the situation. Often in masterclasses we meet experienced leaders who tell us they have been trained over the years to start all hard conversations – but especially feedback conversations – with 'how do *you* think it's going?' What they also tell us is that this doesn't often work out all that well. When the answer is 'how do I think things are going?

Table 3: Clear message key phrases

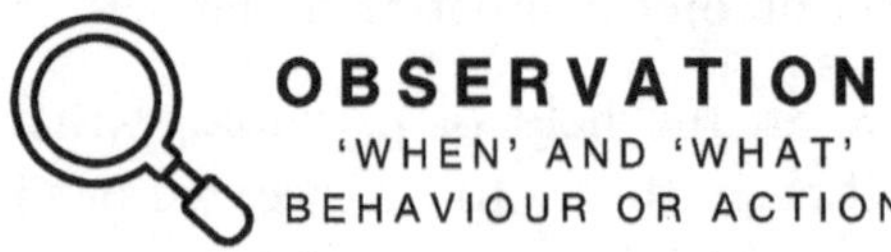

- "In yesterday's meeting I noticed that..."
- "Over the last few weeks I have observed that..."
- "Today it was brought to my attention that..."
- "During your last project I saw that..."

- "This gave the impression that..."
- "This delayed/inhibited/derailed..."
- "This caused confusion/bad feeling/damaged client confidence...."
- "This put pressure on others/reduced efficiency/created work..."
- "This undermined/made others feel/made it difficult to..."

Really well thanks!' it can be very hard to express an opposite view, and then redirect the conversation to some necessary developmental feedback. There can also be a sense of it being a known and inauthentic formula, putting the recipient on the spot to show their hand first, and on edge, as they sense some potentially unwelcome feedback is coming. So whilst we don't advise starting hard conversations in this way, curiosity plays an absolutely vital role in Smart Conflict once you've set the context for the conversation.

The simplest way to increase curiosity, of course, is to ask more questions. Reflect on the balance between the number of questions you ask in relation to the number of statements you make – how can you increase your statement-question ratio?

Putting the framework together so far, here is what Observation, Impact, followed by Curiosity might sound like:

> '*I noticed you interrupted me three times in today's meeting*' (observation), '*so I gave up trying to share the data. I'm worried that you are not in a position to make an informed decision*' (impact). '*What was happening in the conversation from your perspective?*' (curiosity).

High-quality questions

When it comes to demonstrating genuine curiosity, not all questions are equal. Open questions are vastly superior to closed questions. An open question invites expansive answers, encouraging reflection or explanation. They typically start with 'What,' 'How,' 'Why' or 'Tell me about...,' e.g. '*What was happening in the conversation from your perspective?*'

Closed questions generate a brief and specific response, usually 'yes' or 'no.' They typically start with 'Did,' 'Are,' 'Is,' 'Can' or 'Have...,' e.g. '*Did you get what you wanted from the meeting?*' Many of us tend to use a high volume of these kinds of questions, and it's worth noticing the reflex and following up with something more curious and open. Closed questions can be helpful when we are trying to ensure clarity of understanding or moving on from a subject you've explored enough, however, for example: '*I'm hearing that you felt frustrated with the lack of pace of decision making. Is that right?*' but they should be used sparingly.

The primary reason to be curious during a hard conversation is to develop an understanding of the other person's perspectives – their thoughts and feelings on the matter. This is important for three reasons. Firstly, because it gives you more data about the situation. As we discussed earlier in the chapter, our assumptions about the motivations and reasoning of others are often completely, or at least partially, wrong. With a greater understanding of what is going on for them and any other factors which are unknown to you, you can make much better decisions about where to take the conversation next with a much increased chance of an effective outcome. Secondly, because demonstrating curiosity is one of the best ways to signal empathy. We are really trying to see things from where the other person is standing, rather than turning up having drawn all our conclusions already. And thirdly, very often before someone else is willing to listen to us in a hard conversation *we need to have demonstrated having heard them first*.

I'm pretty sure that most of us can think of an argument we've had in the past with a partner, friend or colleague where we felt unheard and misunderstood. What will often happen in that scenario is all our attention will be focused on trying to get our point across, with increasing intensity and emphasis if we tend towards the upper end of the Conflict Styles Scale (i.e. Inflexible or Aggressive) or with a sense of alarm and eventual withdrawal if we tend towards the lower end (i.e. Avoidant or Accommodating). What we aren't doing is listening to the opposing view – we're in defence mode. Once we feel heard and understood it's much easier to listen to a different perspective, even one we disagree with, because there is a sense of equality and fairness. It's that balanced equation of being spoken with, not the imbalance of being spoken at.

Here are some questions that do that well:

'What's your understanding of the situation?'

'What surprises you about what I've just said?'

'Does anything I've said so far feel unfair?'

'What do you need to help us move forward?'

'What ideas or solutions are coming to mind?'

Avoiding 'Why?'

Although it does qualify as an open question starter, it's our consistent observation that '*why?*' questions are experienced as judgemental in tone.[21] When we say 'why?' our sub-text can sound like: '*… because I can't understand for the life of me why you would do something so illogical…*'

'Why did we miss the project deadline?'

'Why are we prioritizing this over other initiatives?'

'Why has engagement dropped in the last quarter?'

All can easily sound accusatory rather than curious. Even if your intention is to understand, starting with a 'why?' can put people on the back foot.

So our advice is to swap 'why' for 'what' or 'how' wherever you can to demonstrate curiosity and a focus on problem solving.

'Why did we miss the project deadline?' becomes *'What factors contributed to us missing the project deadline?'*

'Why are we prioritizing this over other initiatives?' becomes *'How did we decide to prioritize this over other initiatives?'*

'Why has engagement dropped in the last quarter?' becomes *'What might explain a drop in engagement in the last quarter?'*

There's one further useful unlock that comes with a 'how' or 'what' question. Inherent in their framing is an invitation for others to fully explain the thought process that led them to arrive at their current position, allowing us in turn to hear the quality and rigour of their thinking. Some of our thinking doesn't stand up all that well to scrutiny once it's outside of our heads, and having to lay out our thought process clearly exposes this. In this moment a window of opportunity opens – a chance for someone who is steadfast in their fixed position to begin to express doubt in their own conclusions, and move towards a more open position. And open minds are minds that can change.

Getting curious about how someone came to their conclusions is a great tool for those managers and leaders who are struggling with team members who seem totally fixed in their position, for example, in questioning the validity of performance feedback or refusing to carry out an action of which they don't see the point.

The power of summaries

Summaries (delivered by you or the other person) are an excellent way of avoiding the temptation to mind read, and provide a much more reliable way to check your message has landed as intended. You could recap the conversation so far or, even better, ask the other person to summarize what they have taken away.

Some of our clients ask for summaries to be written up via email after the meeting (informally as part of a more formal process) but we'd recommend checking for alignment in the conversation to avoid the common pitfall of realizing, only once you've received the follow-up email, that they've got completely the wrong end of the stick. Now you have to have another conversation that might feel even more awkward, and is certainly going to take up more of your time. As Heidi, a People Partner in Consulting and one of our Smart Conflict Masterclass participants said:

> *'I'll do whatever it takes to ensure I only have to have the conversation once. I've learned the hard way the pain of having to go back because I wasn't clear enough the first time'.*

Sometimes we get pushback on the idea of asking someone to summarize what's been said because '*it feels a bit patronizing*' but the avoidance of misunderstandings and misalignment are worth prioritizing in hard conversations.

Here's some language some of our clients have found works well:

> '*Here's what I've understood from our conversation so far... What are you taking from it?*'
>
> '*It's important to me that I'm clear and I want to check what I meant to say has landed. Could you summarize what you've understood from me so far?*'

Summarizing has more benefits beyond checking for that all important alignment. It also allows us another chance to demonstrate we've been listening, which is a powerful way to build trust in any relationship. Acknowledging what has been shared is also very effective in stopping someone from repeating themselves until they are blue in the face: we only do this when we are not convinced our point has landed. Hearing someone summarize, ideally in their own words, the point we are making is very reassuring and validating, typically heading off (or ending) a rant.

Validate when you don't agree

What can hold us back from summarizing and validating what we've heard, is a fear it might look like we agree, when we don't. It's important to decouple confirming understanding from confirming agreement – they are totally different things. When we validate, we are recognizing or affirming that a person and their feelings or opinions are valid or worthwhile, without sharing whether we fully understand or agree with those feelings or opinions.

Genuine curiosity requires us to hold back our own thoughts and opinions until we have all the information. This is especially important when we disagree, because it will instil confidence that when decisions are made all viewpoints have been considered. Which it turns out – based on hundreds of real client stories – is all most people actually want, even if the decision doesn't go their way.

Here is what validating phrases might sound like:

> *'Here's what I just heard... have I understood correctly?'*
>
> *'So, if I've understood correctly, you wish that...'*
>
> *'So, what you are finding difficult is...'*
>
> *'I can understand how that would be/feel... frustrating/exciting/worrying...'*

Step 5: Action

This last step in the framework is critical when it comes to closing a hard conversation, because it helps to ensure there is a clear roadmap for how any agreed change is going to happen and by when. By clearly agreeing *who* will do *what* by *when* we set up the guardrails for accountability.

Here are some things it's important for you to be clear on in your own mind when initiating the Action step. These are common areas where our clients tend to make mistakes, either by being too indirect or too unspecific. As always, it's worth taking the time to prepare a few bullet points in advance of the conversation if you know there are concrete actions that need to be taken as a result.

Do you have a request, or an instruction? There is a time and place for both, but don't disguise one for the other. Make it clear if there is a non-negotiable.

What's the specific action or behaviour change you need to see? If you don't know this having gone through steps 1–4, you are not ready to agree on actions, and may need to return to the conversation and try again.

How and when will you measure progress/change? How will you both know objectively the change has taken place? When will you check in again, and in what format?

Do you share an understanding of what action needs to happen, by whom and when? Summaries work really effectively here.

Advocating as we do for the power of coaching, in this action step we'd recommend at least beginning with a collaborative approach to generating solutions even if you have a very clear idea of where you want to end up. We know from the neuroscience of behaviour change (see the *Making it stick* chapter for more on this) that the other person is much more likely to take forward actions they have generated themselves, or at least co-generated with you. Very few of us like to be told what to do, so try to keep this as a last resort, and if you do need to give an instruction remember the power of Permission. The more control and autonomy you can give (even if this is limited to the smaller details), the more collaborative it will feel.

When *not* to use the Hard Conversations Framework

There are a few types of conversations where it would be unwise or inappropriate to use the Hard Conversations Framework as a guide and, as ever, we ask you to use your professional judgement and take advice if you're not sure of the right approach. There are some conversations which should be informed by company policy (and/or the law in your country) to ensure fairness and transparency, and avoid potential legal risk – e.g. redundancy, firing, reassignment of roles, disciplinary matters and formal performance improvement procedures – although this list is not exhaustive. There are other hard conversations during which it may only be possible or logical to utilize one or two elements – for example, if you need to impart some difficult company news, you would still aim to get clear on your message, perhaps seek permission for the best time to talk, then get straight into focusing on being empathetic and curious about their reaction and inviting their questions for you, while communicating that the actions from here on may have already been decided. A top tip for landing difficult news is to take the time to reassure on anything that is not changing, and not only focus on what is. The psychological bias of loss aversion means we worry more about what we will lose than what we will gain, and so all our attempts to excite people about, say, the office relocation to a glamourous new location will likely land on deaf ears until they have heard they can still keep their existing hybrid working pattern.[22]

A note on feedback conversations

You can use the Hard Conversations Framework to prepare for most categories of hard conversation, but we want to spend a moment on the most common category which brings people leaders and their organizations to The Power House for support: giving feedback on performance or behaviour.

Why most feedback doesn't work

Research tells us that the way *most* people give unsolicited feedback is completely ineffective if what you are looking for is a *change in behaviour* in the other person.[23] Telling someone what they did wrong is only helpful if they clearly understand the impact of that event, know how to succeed moving forward, and feel motivated to take action. Very often we identify a problem – and frequently one the other person didn't and maybe still doesn't see as problematic themselves – then leave them to work out what, how and when to change. It's not surprising that much of the time this leads to no change, or worse a deterioration of the situation as the feedback has led to demotivation and 'bad feeling,' rather than growth and improvement.

Our clients struggling to have effective feedback conversations with their teams tend to see it falling into two categories:

Negative feedback – i.e. on outcomes, actions or behaviours that are either problematic or not optimal. The hope or expectation is that the receiver will take some kind of corrective action, or change or improve how they approach the situation or task next time.

Positive feedback – i.e. praise, encouragement or reinforcement on how well the receiver did something specific, or their overall performance level. The hope or expectation is that the receiver will be motivated to keep it up, or be given the confidence to dial up their performance even further.

While it's understandable to see things in these binary terms given how feedback training and performance management systems have historically been structured (and how we can sometimes interpret feedback on the receiving end – it's tempting to see it as 'bad' or 'good'), it's not helpful. All feedback should be considered by both the giver and receiver as developmental – that is, its purpose is to support the professional (and sometimes personal) development of the receiver.

Yet how many of us cringe at even the idea of someone saying, 'can I give you some feedback?' The thought of hearing something unexpected about our work performance can be enough to set our heart racing and break out a sweat. Part of this can be the fear that we are about to hear something about ourselves that we'll find painful or embarrassing. Often, we worry we won't know how to respond professionally, or be able to discuss the feedback without being awkward or emotional.

On the other side of that table, many of us dread having to give anything other than resoundingly positive or, at the very least, neutral feedback. One of the most common frustrations we hear from coaching clients about their managers when the relationship has become strained is that they aren't being given any clear or useful feedback on how they are doing or what is expected of them, especially during appraisals or performance reviews which are linked to reward and recognition.

Empty platitudes like 'just keep doing what you're doing!' or 'no particular feedback, everything's good' can feel to the giver like warm and supportive statements, but in effect they are completely useless to the receiver. There's no information about what exactly it is the person is doing that is seen as particularly effective, no insight on where they could improve, and no direction about what is expected from them to meet performance goals. This kind of empty feedback is sometimes the result of complacency or poor management skills, but most often the root cause is the avoidance of giving a piece of difficult but real feedback that might result in a hard but potentially transformational conversation.

If you struggle with feedback – receiving or giving – take comfort. There are some simple ways you can create the conditions for great feedback conversations that feel productive, not hard.

One of the major shifts made by teams and organizations we support in creating an effective feedback culture, is in their collective mindset to thinking of all feedback as a growth opportunity that is going to drive both individual *and* team performance. It doesn't mean that it is always comfortable or easy to hear (or to give). But on the other side of that discomfort is often the insight that builds self-awareness and helps us unlock challenges that have been holding us back, or change the behaviours that might have prevented us from ever making progress.

After one of our Hard Conversations masterclasses, George, now a Senior Partner in a global consulting firm, shared this insight from his early career:

> *'I'll never forget the time when as a junior consultant I was coming back on the plane with Nitin, the practice lead at the time, after a crunch meeting with one of our major clients. As soon as the wheels went up, he turned to me and explained very clearly that the way I had handled telling the client about the problems I had identified was unacceptable. He was understanding – given my relative inexperience – but completely clear in his expectations for next time. I was left without a doubt about how my communication style was coming across. Was it hard to hear? Yep. Was I embarrassed for the rest of the time we were stuck next to each other? If I could have grabbed a parachute and exited via the rear doors, I would have. Am I glad he told me? Definitely.*

But as it was a two hour flight, instead I had to sit with that discomfort and talk about it with Nitin. He was generous enough to share some of the mistakes he'd made as a junior, and what he'd learned from them. He didn't make me feel ashamed – his philosophy was very much about making mistakes being how we learn. I can honestly say that conversation was a turning point in my career. It made me see myself clearly in a way I wasn't able to before – a bit too cocky, too much of a know-it-all, not enough humility – and think about the kind of professional I aspired to be. Actually a lot more like Nitin, who was a master at those client situations. Sharing that he had made plenty of rookie errors when he was in my shoes was an act of generosity I've never forgotten. Now I'm a Partner, I aspire to be as generous in supporting my junior team members. I still look back at it as a conversation that changed everything.'

Help them to get it right, not just tell them what they got wrong

While it's undoubtedly important to be crystal clear about what went wrong/hasn't worked/needs to change, focusing solely on the past can feel excessively negative, and is simply ineffective in supporting development. When giving feedback, move as quickly as possible to what good looks like, and to exploring how you can help the other person to get it right next time. Be specific – both on what needs to change and what good looks like; don't expect them to read your mind or go away and work it out on their own. Ask them for their ideas on what they could do differently and collaborate on coming up with potential solutions.

Ask 'If you got this right, what would that look like?'

Give feedback as close to the event as possible

A core reason that feedback doesn't work is that we leave it days, weeks or – in the case of many company performance review processes – months after the event to raise it. By which time the other person can't remember it, or the significance has been forgotten or lost by one or both of you. While it's not always possible or even desirable to give feedback in the moment (e.g. telling someone their presentation isn't very good right in the middle of it will almost certainly throw them off their stride, and may feel unnecessarily shaming and unkind), a good rule of thumb is to try and raise it verbally within 24 hours or, at the very least, to book within that timeframe the next possible slot to discuss it with them.

Be cautious about giving feedback in written form in the interests of timeliness (e.g. via email, text or instant message) especially if you are raising it for the first time. It doesn't have to be in person – it can even be by phone, but do have a conversation. The tone of voice in written messages can be very hard to correctly interpret, and there's more potential for misunderstanding of your intent. As above, it's good practice to write up formal or significant performance feedback but this should follow a conversation, not replace one.

Giving feedback on behaviour

Paraphrasing the ancient Chinese proverb, we live in interesting times when it comes to workplace norms of behaviour. Things are changing faster than many of us can keep up with. For some, levels of freedom and choice on how, when and where we work evolved to previously unimagined levels for over a decade, only to rapidly begin contracting again as many companies mandated a return to the office in person. What was once – perhaps not very long ago – overlooked or dismissed as a bit of office banter is now definitely not ok, and rightly so. And on the other hand, language and terminology that was until very recently considered to be respectful and intended to be inclusive is considered controversial, inappropriate and in some cases actively prohibited in company communications. The pace of this evolution doesn't seem to be about to slow down any time soon. This can make it hard to navigate conversations about behaviour we personally find problematic, and it's prudent to be very clear about the particular landscape we are in before we open a potentially hard conversation.

Depending on the country in which you are based, the type and size of organization you work for and the type of work you do, there will be varying degrees of structure, policy and legal guidance around acceptable behaviours at work. Some companies have a behaviour charter, but many don't. All this is to say, before you start a conversation about someone's behaviour, be very clear in your mind of the specific examples and the impact the behaviour is having. Check if there's a policy in place and understand if there's an official stance on how to deal with it. If you have a Human Resources department, it will be your first port of call. If there's no policy (or no HR) then check in with your manager, and if you are the boss, do what research you can or take advice on best practice on handling that kind of behaviour in your country or industry before deciding on what course of action to take.

Be clear about boundaries – what's ok, and what's not ok.

The concept of establishing strong personal boundaries has gained a lot of traction in recent years and it is certainly an important thing to consider when thinking about behaviour. To have successful relationships – especially at work – we need to know where the boundaries of desirable, acceptable and unacceptable behaviour lie, for us and for others.

There's a simple formula you can use if you want to try to define for yourself what your personal boundaries are:

- What is ok for me (in terms of my and others' behaviour) in this situation.
- What is *not* ok for me (in terms of my and others' behaviour) in this situation.

Each person will have different personal boundaries. Let's take greetings. Some people are huggers, and will offer everyone a warm hug on meeting, even if for the very first time. While there are those of us who enjoy this show of warmth, or simply feel neutral about it, there are others for whom this would be very uncomfortable indeed. Some people make direct eye contact and offer everyone a firm handshake as their greeting of choice. There are others who find this embarrassingly formal and awkward, or are averse to touching the hands of other people (totally understandable in the post-Covid era). Even in this simple, everyday moment we need to run the gauntlet of establishing and negotiating what is 'ok' for you, and for the other person, in that particular setting.

At work there is another category that's essential to bring in here:

- What's ok for the company (in terms of professional behaviour).
- What's not ok for the company (in terms of professional behaviour).

Sometimes this will be formally written down in values statements and behaviour charters, codified in policy and supported by training so that everyone is clear about what is expected 'around here.' But often what's acceptable or unacceptable is poorly defined, or amorphously part of *the culture* that you might not understand until you get it wrong in some way and it's explained to you clearly. There can also be a gulf between the written values on the website, and the lived values you see from your colleagues in day-to-day working life. Expectations also change over time, across different generations, and with different leaders at the helm.

A lot of the time we are consciously or unconsciously balancing on the intersection of our own personal boundaries and the professional boundaries of expected or tolerated behaviour in our workplace. In some cases, these will be broadly the same. But there are plenty of things we might say or do at home in an unguarded moment or with our friends on a night out that we absolutely would not do (or should not do, anyway) in the office or on a work call with the boss. And coming back to our old friend self-awareness, we might not know we have crossed a boundary or that one even exists until someone tells us. This can be one of the most important kinds of hard conversations in terms of personal and professional development but one of the hardest to navigate. Clients frequently tell us that they give feedback on behaviour – on projects, towards clients, within teams – that are not ok from their perspective, or according to the expectations of the business. But then they get pushback such as:

> *'But I don't think that's a problem. I didn't do anything wrong'*
>
> *'Yes, I did do that. And I'd make the same choice again'*
>
> *'But that's just your view. From my perspective it was the right move'*
>
> *'I was just speaking my truth. It's not my problem if people can't deal with it'*

No thank you. Nothing to see here. And so, they feel stuck about where to go next, back down and let it drop. And the behaviour doesn't change.

Receiving feedback is a skill and not all of us have developed it, so some empathy for this reflexive defensiveness is appropriate. However, one observation we frequently make is that people who push back on behavioural feedback are usually able to very clearly articulate and defend their own personal boundaries, but are less able to recognize or respect those of others in equal measure. And closing that gap of understanding can be the key to unlocking the situation.

It's important to understand both our own *and* others' boundaries. We must know our own, and then take responsibility for managing them. Boundaries are about what we can control ourselves. Think of them as personal commitments that we uphold for ourselves, not demands we make or rules others must follow.

> For example, a boundary sounds like *'I won't check emails after 7pm.'* A demand is: *'You're not allowed to email me after 7pm.'*

Boundaries are our own code of conduct for how we respond, so we must be responsible for holding them consistently ourselves, rather than expecting others to automatically respect them. If someone repeatedly asks us to overstep our boundaries, the action is to adjust our own behaviour, such as declining requests, removing ourselves from situations, or holding and reinforcing the boundary with a simple, firm response.

When we think about our boundaries in this way it can help reduce any frustration or resentment with others (who we feel are not navigating our boundaries effectively), and also remind us that it is our job to create clear expectations for others as to what we are and are not prepared to do or endure.

This is a case where turning the conversation into a Task Conflict (see the *Introduction*) rather than getting into a disagreement about who's right – Relational Conflict – can be very effective. The task being to explore your differing perspectives and develop a greater understanding of how and why you see things differently, then to decide how you move forward. Tactical Empathy (see the tools in *Response*) can be a great way of directing the conversation back to a collaborative place.

Receiving feedback well

One thing that doesn't get an awful lot of attention is how to receive feedback well. Until the happy day that everyone is implementing the Five R model and having hard conversations effectively and consistently you can use the following guidelines to manage those times when you are on the receiving end of some poorly (or just unexpectedly) delivered feedback.

First we need to practice self-compassion and remind ourselves that the ancient part of our brain is hardwired to feel defensive and afraid when someone points out to us that we've fallen short. It's probably never going to feel great, but feeling great is not a useful benchmark for the growth zone. Remember, to be in growth we need a healthy level of challenge, not comfort (see Sanford's Support and Challenge Model in the *Readiness* Chapter).

The practices we want to employ for receiving feedback are all the ones we outline in *Response*: what to do when an unexpected or unwanted hard conversation happens. But here are a few pointers that might help you to gracefully receive unsolicited feedback and turn it into a Smart Conflict opportunity that supports your growth rather than knocking your confidence:

Remember, feedback is data

It's all information. Even if we don't like what we hear and/or we don't agree with it, there will be a reason it's being given. Before you react, lean in to curiosity to really understand what you are being told. If it's not specific enough, ask for examples ('Can you tell me what you've observed specifically?'); if it's not clear what the problem is, then clarify ('Can you clarify what you think the impact of this is, and why you feel it's important?'). All importantly, stay calm (lean on your go-to self-regulation practices, go back to the *Regulation* chapter for a refresher). Hold on to our favourite mantra 'get curious, not furious' if you find yourself thinking feedback is unfair or just plain wrong. Defensiveness will *always* make things worse in feedback conversations. It's fine to disagree, of course, but make it your goal to get into Task Conflict (rather than an argument over who is right) to discover how you and the giver have such different perspectives on the feedback.

Asking for feedback

One sure fire way to reduce the amount of unsolicited feedback we receive is to ask for more feedback more regularly. Doing this puts you back in the driving seat, and focuses feedback on your identified development areas (since you are dictating what you ask for feedback on). Even better than asking for feedback, is to ask for what Marshall Goldsmith – the business educator and coach – coined 'Feedforward.'[24] Feedforward shifts the focus from what went wrong in the past to what can be improved in the future. Instead of critiquing past performance, it offers constructive, actionable ideas and suggestions for moving forward. The technique is simple: think of an area that you'd like to improve on, then ask your manager or colleagues for two or three actionable things you could do or try to get better. Don't argue or dismiss what you've already tried, simply say thank you and decide what to implement.

Readiness summary

- **Readiness is essential for navigating hard conversations; it involves preparing both your mindset and energy ('being') and your strategy and tools ('doing').**
- **Not every hard conversation needs to happen; use the Smart Conflict decision tree to assess whether it's the right time and whether you're the right person to have it.**
- **Anticipatory anxiety is often worse than the event itself, and techniques like CBT, scenario planning and exposure can reduce fears and build your resilience.**
- **Kindness includes empathy and honesty. Using high support combined with high challenge supports others' growth, which often requires communicating hard truths.**
- **The Five-Step Hard Conversations Framework (Permission, Observation, Impact, Curiosity, Action) offers a clear structure for difficult conversations.**
- **Feedback should be developmental, not just praise or critique, delivered close to the event, and be future-focused to be actionable and effective.**
- **Boundaries are personal responsibilities, not demands on others. Managing them with clarity and ownership reduces resentment and confusion.**

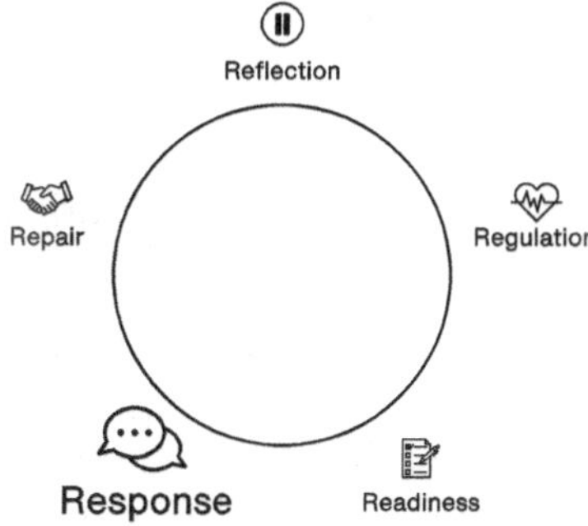

8

Response

'You cannot reason with a tiger when your head is in its mouth.' –
Winston Churchill[1]

In this chapter we walk you through what to do when, despite the best laid plans, you find yourself in the middle of an unexpected conversation with no idea what to do or say next. Mastering the ability to choose your response strategically rather than being at the mercy of impulse is a worthwhile pursuit in any area of your life. A considered response not only reduces the risk of your blundering in and causing some kind of unintended damage – reputational, relational or operational – but it greatly increases your chances of creating an outcome you do want.

As with most of Smart Conflict, mastering your response isn't complicated. The techniques we share are simple to learn and implement but they take some practice before they feel natural and instinctive. Conflict-coaching clients often ask how some leaders make it look so easy to keep their cool in the face of a barrage of negative questions. More than once, an HR leader who has engaged us to run a group conflict-coaching session has rushed up at the end to ask how we manage to stay good humoured in the face of the challenging behaviour that unfolded in the previous hours. The answer in both cases is intentionality and experience. If you intend to stay calm and focus on solving for the outcome and relationship you want to create, practice and experience will do the rest. But we all have to start somewhere. So if you know your biggest stretch in hard conversations is knowing how to respond, this is the chapter for you. If you know you struggle to stay calm, head back to the *Regulation* chapter to find some go-to practices to help you regulate your nervous system in the moment.

A note on managing risks

Managing physical risks

At work (as in all areas of our life) we need to take responsibility for keeping ourselves and others safe in body and mind. If there is the slightest chance your frustration or anger could escalate into anyone getting physically hurt, our simple recommendation is to remove yourself from that situation as a matter of urgency and create as much distance between you and the potential target of your wrath as possible. Get your coat and go home, if that's what it takes. This might seem far-fetched, but we have supported a number of organizations where one poke of the bear too far has resulted in two grown men swinging for each other over the boardroom table, and a particularly memorable episode of one karate-loving colleague roundhouse kicking another at the office party after a petty disagreement about a contract. Bad things can happen when emotions run high.

If you feel at risk of physical threat from someone else at work, our emphatic recommendation is the same: remove yourself from the situation as quickly and calmly as you can. Don't try to reason or argue with someone who has become aggressive – politely excuse yourself and leave before things can escalate further. Claire, a coaching client who had recently joined a medium-sized construction company as their new head of procurement told us the following story, illustrating how quickly things can get out of hand:

'I had handled a Request for Proposals for a new project and shortlisted suppliers according to my standard process, and informed everyone who hadn't been selected. Dave – a long time contractor who was used to the previous informal appointment arrangements – was absolutely furious he hadn't been given the work, and sent me a barrage of abusive emails. While the CEO agreed I should stick to the process, he told me I had to handle Dave personally and give him a face to face explanation one-to-one. Dave was a childhood friend of the CEO's wife and a regular dinner party guest, and the situation was creating tension for him at home.

As soon as Dave arrived in the meeting room, he slammed his fists on the desk and shouted aggressively that I didn't know who I was dealing with. I tried to explain calmly and reasonably, but he wouldn't let me speak. His tone was so threatening. I was terrified, honestly. In the end he stormed out swearing. Thankfully his behaviour was witnessed by a passing teammate and was enough evidence to get him barred as a supplier, but it's not too strong a word to say it was traumatic. I decided I had to resign a week later. It doesn't feel like a safe environment to be a procurement professional.'

In supporting Claire to feel able to handle future potential conflicts, we helped her revisit the event and plan and practise her exit strategies, in the sincere hope she wouldn't ever need to use them again (it goes without saying that the above scenario is completely unacceptable on a number of fronts). These included using a prepared phrase as soon as she noticed the aggressive tone: 'Dave, this behaviour/this aggressive tone/that offensive word is unacceptable to me. I am ending the meeting here.' and immediately leaving the room, getting herself to safety and discreetly informing building security and HR of the situation so it could be escalated (to the police, if necessary). While we do want you to lean into the right kinds of conversations, we would never suggest you persevere in the face of obvious outward aggression. Above all, keep yourself and others safe from harm.

Managing psychological risks

The psychological and mental health risks of hard conversations can be less visible but potentially more complex to navigate. As we learned in the *Reflection* chapter, we all have different 'default' settings when it comes to conflict. Some of us are very resilient to robust debate and brush off cross words easily, while others find even a slightly heightened tone alarming. If you follow the Five Rs when initiating hard conversations, you will be well on your way to creating an environment which feels psychologically safe for others in your presence, and you will certainly be leaning in to creating awareness of and having curiosity about what others need to be in growth rather than anxiety.

However, there will always be factors you can't be aware of – particular sensitivities or personal circumstances that are affecting working life, even the simple fact of someone having a really bad day. If you need to have a hard conversation but sense the other person may be feeling too fragile to respond well – and especially if they tell you that they don't feel able to handle it – then in most cases it's the right decision to delay. It doesn't mean that you don't have the conversation at all, but postponing to a mutually agreed time and potentially making some adjustments to how and where the meeting takes place can make a big difference to how it lands. If in doubt about how to handle a conversation when you know (or just sense) that the other person is struggling, get advice from HR, or there are some great online resources (e.g. mind.org.uk has some helpful guides on mental health at work).

Some organizations we work with have what might be characterized as a default Aggressive communication style on our conflict scale day-to-day, expressed in the way in which colleagues interact with each other: direct, honest, competitive, passionate (this is distinct from being threatening or physically aggressive). This seems to be particularly common in some sectors (e.g. financial services and law) but it's certainly not as straightforward as being industry specific. Not everyone who is operating in an Aggressive communication culture would experience this as problematic, and some people positively thrive on it. There can certainly be pros when it comes to directness, clarity and honesty. If you join this kind of culture and you want to be heard and have an impact, adopting an aggressive style yourself might be the only way to succeed. We also work with many businesses who pride themselves on being gentle, kind and caring with one another, whose employees would be horrified to encounter those more aggressive cultures, but are often struggling with their team growth and performance as they are avoiding hard conversations altogether. So when one person's aggressiveness is another person's directness, and one person's kindness is another person's evasiveness, navigating and maintaining psychological safety at work for ourselves and others can feel very confusing.

For this reason it's important that your team and wider organization develop a shared understanding of the boundaries and behaviours that are and are not acceptable at your place of work, especially for 'how we do hard conversations and conflict around here'. These behavioural agreements will greatly vary from one organization to another so it's important not to assume everyone is on the same page. For a very practical guide to how to design a behavioural charter (as well as a wealth of other tools and techniques for high-performing teams) we highly recommend getting hold of a copy of *Building Top Performing Teams* by Lucy Widdowson and Paul Barbour.[2]

Responding when things get derailed: Tools and techniques

So far in this book we've shared tools and frameworks you can use to ensure things do not escalate and reduce the chances of misunderstandings happening. But sometimes things don't go to plan, and we might find ourselves in hard conversations that feel very far from Smart Conflict. In this instance the single best de-escalation strategy involves regulating yourself first (see the *Regulation* chapter for practical ways to do this), diffusing the tension, then redirecting the conversation productively.

In this section we share some of our and our clients' favourite tools for getting things back on track when they've headed in the wrong direction.

Get curious, not furious

When we are surprised by an unexpected conversation, some disappointing news or by someone else's negative reaction to our well-intentioned feedback, our automatic emotional response can be surprisingly strong. Irritation, frustration, hurt or anger can rise to the surface and override our best intentions to be calm and collected. Our emotional intelligence can be overridden in an instant by what psychologist Daniel Goleman called 'amygdala hijack' as the brain prioritizes survival instincts over logical reasoning, leading to impulsive decisions, outbursts or panic.[3]

If you find yourself gripped by a strong emotion in the midst of a hard conversation, consciously remind yourself of this trigger phrase: 'get curious, not furious.' Then, follow these steps:

1) **Generate internal curiosity**: Mindfully notice the sensations in your body – where are you feeling the emotion? Your chest, arms, stomach, legs?

   What's the nature of the sensation – tight, pulsing, hot, cold, sharp, dull?

   What label would you give to the emotion – is it anger, or really sadness? Is it frustration, or disappointment?

   The simple act of getting curious about your emotional response and putting some language around it, switches on your prefrontal cortex (the logical, thinking brain) and begins to dampen the amygdala response.

2) **Create external curiosity**: when in doubt about what to do or say next, ask an open question, or find another way to get the other person to open up further. For example, if

surprised by some feedback, you could say: 'I'm surprised to hear that, could you say more so I can understand' or 'can you give me some examples to illustrate what you mean?' Asking questions in this way serves two purposes: it buys you more time to think and regulate yourself before responding, and it gives you more information about what's being discussed, allowing you to make better decisions.

If you are so surprised that you can't even formulate a question, the highly respected coach Michael Bungay Stanier suggests having a prepared phrase for such situations that signals your curiosity with warmth and goodwill. His go-to phrase is 'How fascinating!' delivered with an expansive hand gesture and a sincere smile.[4] And while not everyone can pull that off (tone is everything – we're not going for sarcastic here, but genuine curiosity), finding a phrase that works for you can create just enough of a gap between stimulus and response to allow you to gather your composure and choose your next question.

3) **Be curious about intent**: misunderstandings are common, particularly when our emotions run high, and a good rule of thumb is to notice your reaction to what you think is happening, and then to check for understanding before choosing your response. If you're on the receiving end of something that you've found upsetting, try to assume positive intent before responding, and play back to them what you've heard to check if that was the intended message.

   If someone reacts poorly to something you have said, ask them to summarize what they heard – this might explain their response and you then have the opportunity to clarify your intended message and correct any misunderstanding.

The power of a pause

Having a high-quality debate requires both parties to be engaged and feel there is value in hearing and being heard. Without these in place, and heightened emotions in play, you might be better off just taking time out. Taking as little as 10 minutes away from the conversation before rejoining can create surprisingly big shifts in the dynamic, and unlock even the most entrenched positions. Sometimes a little more time is needed, and you might choose to re-group on another day. But we'd recommend trying the 10-minute break first, because it might just do the trick.

As coaches and mediators we have worked with many pairs (and sometimes whole teams) of senior executives in scenarios where communications are tense, collaboration has halted and all trust has evaporated. In many cases this has persisted for a year or more before they reach our consulting rooms. Frequently, an hour or so into a mediation session, someone might say: '*I'm sorry but I don't think we're getting anywhere*'. When we hear this signalled loss of hope we suggest taking the 10-minute break. Everyone grabs a coffee, goes for a walk, takes some deep breaths in another room, stares into the distance, goes back to their email… it doesn't really matter how it's spent, what is important is the pause. Without fail, when we re-start the conversation something has always changed, and the majority of the time, a completely different (usually more productive) conversation ensues. Something really magical happens in that pause as it opens up an opportunity for everyone to step back and reflect on the bigger picture, and the outcome they're looking to achieve. Time and time again, we see people return ready for the first time to own their part in things, and be more empathetic, open and direct.

You can instigate a pause in a hard conversation by simply proposing: '*I feel like a break would be useful. Can we take a 10-minute pause and come back to this?*'

Create your prepared responses

By creating a prepared response we are not only able to ensure we say something instead of nothing, we are also reducing our chances of saying or doing something we later regret, at best because it was ineffective, at worst because it escalated things or created reputational risk for us. If we know that we have a tendency for strong emotional responses in these contexts (e.g. tears, anger, freezing) it can be especially helpful to have a set of planned phrases up your sleeve.

We've identified four types of prepared response that our clients have found most helpful: The Primer, The Opener, The Breather and The Closer.

The Primer: Primes the other person (and you) for exactly what you want to talk about. You can do this by email, phone or in person, in advance, or in the moment.

Example: '*I wanted to talk with you about Thursday's presentation. When would be a good time to do that together?*'

The Opener: How you plan to open the conversation. Creating a positive emotional tone and environment for connection and trust (sometimes referred to as 'resonance').

Example: '*I really value our working relationship, and because of that, I want to have an open conversation about something that's been challenging for me.*'

The Breather: A go-to phrase when you don't know what to say, and want to buy yourself some time before responding.

Example: '*I wasn't expecting this, let me take a moment/day to gather my thoughts.*' (Can also be used as an emergency closer if things take a challenging turn.)

The Closer: The closer can function as a 'bid' for repair and goodwill in the relationship (a positive close).

Example: '*Thanks for this conversation. I know it wasn't easy, but I really value our ability to have these discussions.*'

The key to pre-prepared responses is to find language and phrases that feel natural for you, but we hope these bring to life the theory so you can play around and find your own key phrases.

Use tactical empathy

In his well-known book *Never Split the Difference* (which we highly recommend for a deep dive on negotiation strategies in conflict situations), former FBI hostage negotiator Chris Voss introduces the concept of Tactical Empathy, which he believes is central to his and his colleagues' success in resolving hostage situations.[5] This technique can be very useful (at work and elsewhere) when you encounter a conversation where you find yourself unable to relate to the other person's perspective or values; or you both have entrenched positions and have reached an impasse on how to move forward.

Tactical Empathy involves understanding and recognizing the emotions, perspectives and motivations of the other person, without necessarily agreeing with them, to build trust and guide the conversation towards the desired outcome. This is different to the way we usually think about showing empathy, which involves demonstrating a degree of emotional resonance with the other person or trying to show you understand how they feel.

In this scenario you might not understand how they feel or where they are coming from at all. You might not feel an iota of emotional empathy – just confused, annoyed or angry. The trick here is not to get hooked by your own emotional response and instead get deeply curious about how the other person is seeing the world (or the specific situation at hand) so differently to you, with the aim of gaining genuine understanding and to make sure the other person feels fully heard, even if you are finding it hard to see their perspective.

As usual, open questions (i.e. questions that can't easily be answered with a simple yes or no) are the best way of demonstrating curiosity and encouraging the other person to speak. This is where you can start really leaning into Tactical Empathy. While sometimes all you can do is 'fake it 'til you make it', really try and generate real curiosity, even fascination, about where the other person is coming from and how you see things so differently. For example, for a difficult feedback conversation you might try:

> *'It sounds like we have very different perspectives on the importance of this feedback. Can you tell me more about why you don't think it's something we should be focusing on?'*
>
> *'It sounds like you're feeling a bit surprised by this. Can you share your thoughts?'*
>
> *'Can you say more about why you disagree with Annabel's feedback on Friday's meeting?'*
>
> *'Can you talk me through what happened on Friday from your perspective so I can understand the full picture?'*
>
> *'Can you help explain what I might be missing when it comes to this situation so I can better understand?'*

Once they have explained and you feel you have understood (even if you still don't agree), demonstrate having heard them by summarizing their position and checking your understanding using phrases like:

> *'So what I'm hearing is… Have I understood that correctly?'*
>
> *'What I understand from what you have said is… Have I got that right?'*
>
> *'My understanding is that your perspective is… Is that right? Is there anything else I need to know before we move on?'*

If it turns out you haven't understood them correctly, or they have more to say before they feel they have been heard, ask more open questions and re-check that you have a shared understanding.

These kinds of conversations sometimes take more than one meeting. And while it can seem (sometimes frustratingly) time consuming, doing the hard work here to get on the same page will save you a lot of time downstream as it will help prevent the situation escalating or repeating. Having explored and gained a better understanding of their position and explained your and/or the business' position clearly too, you can still be inflexible about the message you need to land, and the behaviour change you need to see. But the chances are you will understand each other better and the other person will be more able to listen, having been heard (even if you still don't agree with what they've said, and they don't necessarily agree with you). From this position it's much easier to return to the Task – e.g. what do we do to move forward so this doesn't happen again? – than from a position of trying to argue your point with someone who views things very differently to you.

Troubleshooting

Sometimes you just need some simple advice when things go wrong. Table 4 provides a quick reference guide for how to manage some of the most frequent challenges we get asked about in hard conversations.

Table 4: Troubleshooting crib sheet

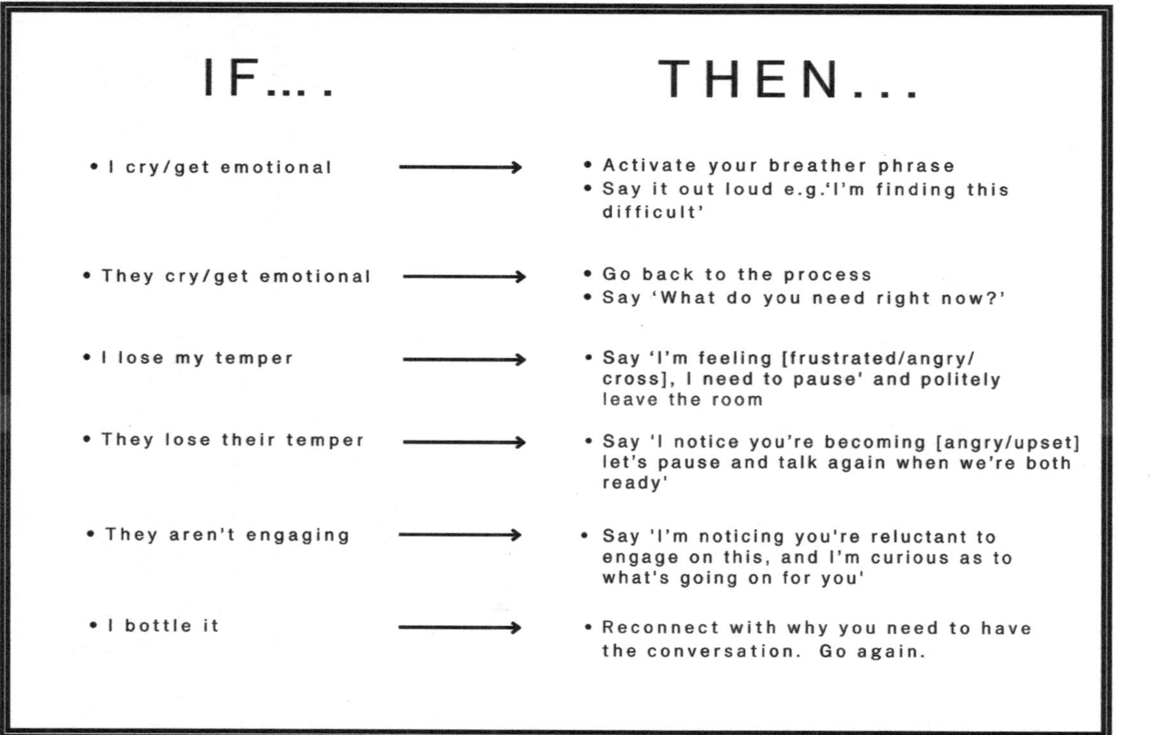

IF....		THEN...
• I cry/get emotional	→	• Activate your breather phrase • Say it out loud e.g.'I'm finding this difficult'
• They cry/get emotional	→	• Go back to the process • Say 'What do you need right now?'
• I lose my temper	→	• Say 'I'm feeling [frustrated/angry/cross], I need to pause' and politely leave the room
• They lose their temper	→	• Say 'I notice you're becoming [angry/upset] let's pause and talk again when we're both ready'
• They aren't engaging	→	• Say 'I'm noticing you're reluctant to engage on this, and I'm curious as to what's going on for you'
• I bottle it	→	• Reconnect with why you need to have the conversation. Go again.

Reasons to hang in there when it feels hard

As Ryan Holiday argues in his book *The Obstacle Is the Way*, challenges and setbacks are not just opportunities for growth, they are the path to getting what you want.[6] Hanging in there when a conversation feels hard is worthwhile because the sharing of hard truths, as uncomfortable as they are, is the gateway to growth and deeper, more trusting relationships. It's also the path to de-risking critical decisions, and solving hard problems. Avoiding tough discussions may feel easier in the moment, but unresolved tensions linger, erode trust and often resurface in more damaging ways. The real risk isn't the discomfort you might endure, it's what happens when you avoid hard conversations. Or, as we often say, when it comes to conflict, time doesn't heal, it hardens.

So we want you to choose long-term gains over short-term comfort. The more you have hard conversations, the more you will build your resilience in having them, and the more you will reap the benefits of more resilient and accountable teams around you. You just need to be prepared.

Response summary

- **It's important to be aware of managing risks in conflict at work – reputational, psychological and sometimes physical – and scenario plan accordingly.**
- **When you are planning a potentially hard conversation, having some prepared responses if things get derailed can greatly increase the chances of success.**

- **Prepared responses include techniques, such as increasing your ratio of open questions or taking a pause if things get heated.**
- **Tactical Empathy can be a useful strategy to get back into Task Conflict when things have begun to take a turn towards Relational Conflict.**
- **You can prepare forms of words in advance to use in different scenarios, including having a 'rip cord' phrase when you need to elegantly exit or give yourself time to think, such as 'I wasn't expecting to have this conversation, I'll need some time to reflect so I can give you a considered response.'**

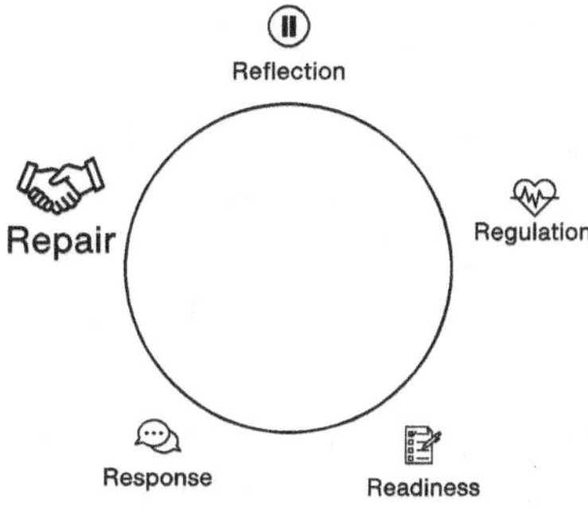

9

Repair

'The wound is the place where the light enters.' – Rumi[1]

Although we absolutely believe that all five of the Rs are important, and to be skilled at Smart Conflict it's necessary to have a good understanding of each individually as well as how they work together, if we had to choose the one that has the potential to be the most transformational, it would be *Repair*.

It's our experience that working relationships can survive a lot more conflict than most people fear. And on the other side of that conflict can be amazing things – new learning, growth, increased trust and connection, innovation, unimagined positive change. But to reap those benefits we must make sure we repair the damage (known in relationship research as 'rupture') that the hard conversations and the feelings that arose around them may have caused. We need to literally *make a repair* to the relationship through our words, gestures or actions – in some cases, all three.

Repair it with liquid gold

Kintsugi (金継ぎ) is the Japanese art of repairing broken pottery with lacquer mixed with powdered gold, silver or platinum. Instead of hiding the cracks, Kintsugi highlights them, embracing imperfection as part of the object's history. We think this is a lovely analogy for human relationships – the breakage and repair become part of their story, rather than something to disguise. Those new seams of gold, silver or platinum symbolize how going through those challenges makes the relationship even stronger and more valuable. Take a moment to think about the relationships that have been most important and meaningful to you over your life. The ones where the trust has been highest. These won't have been free of difficulty or misunderstandings, but the chances are you will have worked to overcome them and learned something about yourself and the other person from the experience, creating a better understanding between you.

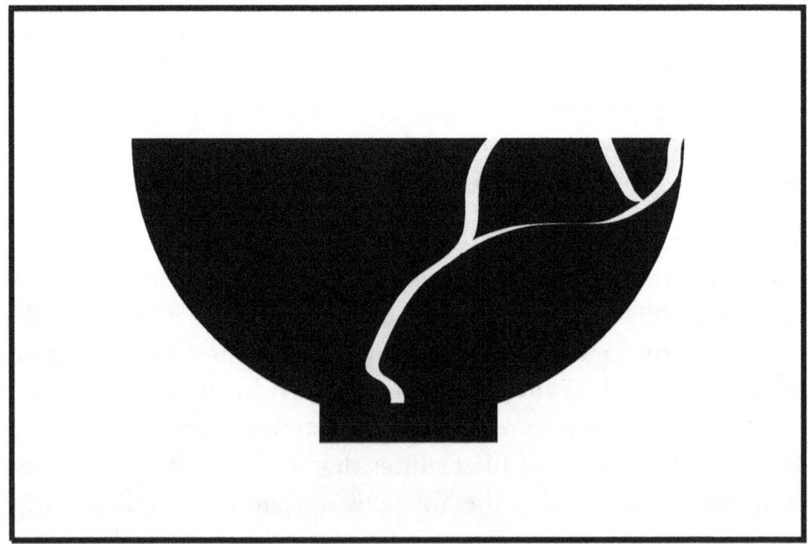

Figure 7: Kintsugi pottery bowl

When it comes to conflict, time doesn't heal. It hardens

It's true that the way we behave at work is often different from how we behave at home, with our family or with our closest friends. While there are of course exceptions, in many cultures the rules of 'professionalism' we have been taught or have internalized through our experience often encourage us to maintain a distance from others we work with, and keep ourselves to ourselves. Or, at the very least, be wary of crossing the line into being overly familiar or giving too much of our real selves away unless we are completely sure of our ground. Even the idea of having 'work friends' can be surprisingly controversial. There are those who think work and friendship don't mix, as the blurred boundaries make things too complicated, especially when people are at different levels of seniority or potentially competing for limited promotions.

There are also those who think there is no place for emotion at work. This is unrealistic and misguided. As we learned in *Regulation*, it's neither possible nor desirable to be emotion-free. While it's the responsibility of each one of us to manage our behaviour according to the setting, our instinctive responses like fear, anxiety and anger are part of what keeps us safe; and positive emotions such as excitement, empathy, connection to others, even love (for your job or for your team) are an important part of what makes work feel worth doing. However, it can be hard to assess someone else's tolerance for emotion or comfort levels with 'talking it out', and there are those that make it clear that they'd rather walk over hot coals than have a heart-to-heart with someone at work.

All this potential complicatedness – coupled with power imbalances and the fear of making a mistake that costs us professionally, then mixed with our own default conflict settings – can mean that when we experience a disagreement or falling out with a colleague or client we can feel like the best thing we can do is pull further away from the other person, rather than going towards them to repair the damage. Unfortunately, sustained avoidance tends to make things worse, not better.

What counts as rupture in working relationships?

It's not only the major ruptures that count – arguments, raised voices, cross words and big emotions. The small moments of disconnection, misattunement or bad feeling between us can cause multiple tiny fractures that lead to major cracks in the relationship. The types of rupture you may experience in working relationships (but indeed any relationship) fall into categories such as:

Confrontation: e.g. arguments, criticism, expressions of anger or frustration.

Withdrawal: e.g. avoidance, emotional or physical distancing, 'the silent treatment'.

Misattunement: e.g. dismissiveness, not being acknowledged, misunderstanding, hurt feelings that go unnoticed.

Unspoken: e.g. lack of responsiveness, passive resistance, misaligned expectations/assumptions, unspoken resentment.

Dynamic: e.g. micromanagement, perceived disrespect, being undermined, power imbalance, imposition of an agenda.

Breach: e.g. broken trust, rejection, betrayal, dishonesty.

It's often the case that a conflict at work derives from a thousand cuts rather than a single blow. When we are on the inside of a conflict it can be difficult and sometimes bewildering to unpick where things have gone wrong. But as you can see from the examples above, ruptures can be small and varied in type. Minor but repetitive breaks in connection that add up to relationship breakdown.

What gets in the way of repair?

You might be thinking, 'well, obviously you need to fix things after you've fallen out with someone at work' and yes, on the surface, it sounds obvious. Most of us know we should say sorry if we think we've been in the wrong. But the cycle of rupture and repair is more nuanced than disagreements and apologies and, as we know from the fundamentals of Smart Conflict, thinking in binary terms of who's right and who's wrong has the potential to keep us in Relational (Destructive) Conflict rather than help us out of it and into a constructive place. We need to keep the quality of the relationship in mind, and the balance of overall positive and negative, supportive and challenging interactions over time.

There are many reasons why we don't attempt to repair relationships when there's been a rupture of some kind. Sometimes it's because we don't realize a rupture has occurred. Sometimes it's because we don't care – either because the relationship isn't important enough, or we're past the point of trying to fix it.

However, the most common reason our clients and masterclass participants give us for failing to make a repair to a working relationship is that it's all a bit *awkward*. As we learned in *Reflection*, there are many things that influence our default responses to conflict and hard conversations. If you tend towards Avoidant or Aggressive as your default, it's likely that after a hard conversation with a colleague (especially one which has been emotional, stressful or didn't end well) you will most likely think things like:

> *'I'll just give him some space and leave him alone for a while'*
>
> *'Time heals – it's best not to bring it up again'*

And no doubt, this is with the best of intentions in the hope that things will get better if left well alone. However, in practice this leads to behaviour that increases the size of the rupture rather than healing it. Giving someone 'time and space' tends to involve versions of avoiding or ignoring them, which can generate feelings of embarrassment, shame, even rejection. All of which are types of rupture in themselves.

Remembering the importance of *Regulation*, there are of course situations when everyone needs time to cool off, and taking a bit of time to do it is a wise strategy. But we'd say as a rule of thumb not to leave it more than 24 to 48 hours after the event to make what is called a 'bid for repair' – signalling to the other person you'd like to make it ok with them in some way.

Learning to repair: Remember, not everyone thinks like you

> *'I think I'll just have to quit. I'm just so hurt and confused about the situation. Suki and I used to have what I thought was a great working relationship. I really thought she was a friend. I don't know what it is that I've done wrong, but she's become so cold and transactional with me. We did have different views on the marketing strategy, which was the first time we've not agreed about something. We didn't even argue. But since then, it's like she's pulled up the drawbridge on me. I can tell she's trying to avoid me, and only gives one sentence answers to my texts and instant messages. She's not being rude as such, but I feel completely frozen out. I have no idea what she's saying about me to the rest of the leadership team but they also seem to have changed how they are with me, and it's making me so anxious. I wish I could go back in time and do something differently, but I can't see what I did that was so bad. What can I do?'*

Aida, a Senior Director in a medical technology firm, came into coaching due to the stress of a relationship breakdown with Suki, a peer on the leadership team who – until recently – she had considered a friend. Aida had loved her job and was doing great work by all measures but was on the verge of resigning as she felt so alienated and exposed by the sudden and unexplained coldness of Suki, and the shift it had caused in the dynamics with the rest of the team. We suggested that before quitting, Aida consider a facilitated conversation with Suki to see if we could unravel what had gone wrong and help them to move forward. Aida agreed to it and their manager proposed it to Suki who, although surprised, accepted the invitation.

Louise interviewed Aida and Suki separately to understand their perspectives, before bringing them together to discuss what had gone wrong and to make agreements on how to move forward. As is often the case, it soon emerged from the individual interviews that their approach to conflict – and their tolerance for disagreement – were very different.

From Suki's perspective, Aida had reacted emotionally to the way the new strategy would impact her team. She said Aida had become frustrated and then tearful when Suki pushed back on her objections. Suki explained:

> *'That was enough for me. I don't do emotions at work. I also don't do guilt trips. I don't have time for drama. We just need to get on with it. I've no idea why she's taken it so personally. I'd never seen this side of her. I've given her space to get over it but she's still sulking. I'm shocked she wants to leave because of that! It was nothing, a complete overreaction. These things happen all the time. It's business.'*

From Aida's perspective, Suki had started the meeting about the new strategy being her usual, friendly self, but as soon as Aida started to question some of the implications Suki suddenly became cold and dismissive. She elaborated:

> *'It was all smiles until I started to ask questions about the knock-on effects on my team. She kept saying that it was the right call, the team would be fine, and we just needed to get on with it. I tried a few different ways of approaching it but eventually she just snapped that we'd have to agree to disagree on this one. She ended the video call without saying goodbye. Since then, she's barely said a word to me. My team has to work closely with Suki's and I can't work under these conditions, it's too stressful. Every time we are in a meeting it's so unpleasant, she just ignores me.'*

Neither Aida nor Suki had tried to approach the other on the subject since that meeting, which had taken place eight weeks before. Instead, over that time they had both allowed their separate interpretations of the other's response to blow what was a relatively minor difference of opinion into a significant conflict. They also hadn't dealt with the downstream effects of the new strategy on Aida's team – which were indeed significant. The team were feeling unsupported, and their performance was hindered by the uncertainty of direction. Aida's avoidance of addressing the situation was translating into a lack of leadership, and a tense 'us vs them' dynamic had developed with Suki's team, who were receiving no guidance from Suki on how to manage the objections and resistance coming from Aida's camp.

Having a better understanding of their positions, Louise brought Aida and Suki together for two joint conversations. In the first, she facilitated them to listen to each other as they explained what they had experienced during that meeting, and what they had felt in the weeks since. As the stories unfolded, it became clear to both of them that Aida found conflict of any kind very stressful, and needed a lot of reassurance that everything was ok after cross words were had. It was also clear that Suki had a high tolerance for conflict, could brush off disagreements easily and didn't ruminate on them afterwards. It came as a revelation to Suki that Aida – also a seasoned and serious professional – didn't have that reflex. She didn't realize that Aida was *hurt*. Suki thought she was being manipulative. Aida was surprised to hear how little Suki had thought about the disagreement since – in her mind she'd moved on and was waiting for Aida to 'get over it', but without any malice. And this realization proved the key to unlocking the conflict between them.

In the next joint conversation, Louise guided Aida and Suki to make some agreements about how and when they would return to the unresolved issues on the strategy, and how they would communicate in future, recognizing their differing needs and reflexes in response to hard conversations. An important step was committing to some new ways of responding for both of them. In Aida's case, these centred on better regulation when she felt stressed, and being aware of a tendency to catastrophize rather than collaborate when under pressure, leading to being *Avoidant* in crunch moments. Suki committed to being more curious and compassionate when experiencing pushback from others, and to consciously move between Conflict Styles during hard conversations, aiming to arrive as *Collaborative* as often as possible rather than defaulting to *Inflexible* as soon as she encountered resistance. And both of them made commitments to follow up to make a repair when there had been a rupture, even (or especially) if it felt awkward for both of them to have that kind of conversation. To lean into the discomfort, rather than away, and learn new ways of choosing to respond to conflict.

Louise invited them to say anything else that needed to be said to allow them to repair and move on. Aida expressed how important her working relationship with Suki had been to her enjoyment of her role before the disagreement, and how much it would mean to her to be able to return to how things had been. Suki – who in her own words didn't 'do emotions at work' – burst into tears, unexpectedly touched. The power of repair can be wonderful to witness, and even better to receive.

If you are in a conflict at work which you are struggling to understand (or have been in one in the past), head back to the *Reflection* chapter now to explore your own default conflict settings using our *Conflict Styles Scale*, and to the exercise on mapping Unmet Needs in relationships – yours and others. See if what you discover gives you the clues you need on how you could begin to make a repair.

How repair happens: The rupture to repair ratio

> *'Successful relationships are not about avoiding conflict, but about knowing how to repair after conflict.'* – John Gottman[2]

Research in 2020 by developmental psychologists Ed Tronick and Claudia Gold into human attachment indicates that even in healthy relationships, perfect attunement (total harmony) between two people occurs only about 30% of the time. The remaining 70% of the time comprises varying degrees of misattunement (rupture) and the subsequent repair.[3] In their book *The Power of Discord*, Tronick and Gold, leading experts on human attachment, argue that perfect harmony in relationships is neither necessary nor possible. Instead, relationships naturally go through cycles of connection, disconnection (rupture) and reconnection (repair) – a process that builds resilience, trust and deeper understanding.

So, in that context, how much repair do we need to make for each rupture? And how do we do it?

The good news is that repair doesn't have to involve grand gestures, huge amounts of time or a trained professional. But it does need a level of commitment and consistency, and what kind and how much repair is required will depend on two things: the magnitude of the rupture, and the quality of the relationship (e.g. the levels of harmony, trust, respect and liking) that existed *before* it took place. In the section on The Marble Jar below we'll look at how the relationship can be built to withstand inevitable ruptures.

According to the renowned relationship researchers Dr. John and Dr. Julie Gottman, a good rule of thumb, however, is to think about rupture and repair in terms of a 5:1 ratio. For each rupture (i.e. an interaction which was perceived as negative or damaging by one or both people), five 'bids for repair' (i.e. interactions that signal a desire to reconnect, or demonstrate warmth and liking) are needed to get the relationship back to where it was before.[4]

The Gottmans define bids for repair as any efforts to de-escalate tension and reconnect after conflict. These are verbal or non-verbal gestures that one person makes to reduce negativity, restore emotional connection and prevent escalation. The success of a relationship is strongly tied to how often and effectively each party recognizes and responds to these repair attempts. If one person responds positively to another's bid for repair, this is a first step in restoring the relationship. However, if they ignore or reject the other's bid for repair, then further attempts are needed. If continued bids for repair are not accepted, this is where relationship breakdown tends to occur.

The definitive, ideal rupture-to-repair ratio in human relationships is still the subject of some debate, and rupture and repair in working relationships in particular is little studied to date – disappointing given the serious impact of conflict at work. Gottman's primary source for the 5:1 ratio was a study of thousands of married couples, but some research indicates the 5:1 ratio also extends to workplace relationships. For example, in 2004, Marcial Losada and Emily Heaphy examined the impact of positive-to-negative interaction ratios on team performance. They observed that high-performing teams maintained a ratio of approximately 5.6 positive interactions for every negative one.[5] Other thinkers like the psychologist Barbara Fredrickson suggest that based on what we know about the conditions for healthy attachment (see the *Reflection* chapter for more on attachment styles), a 3:1 ratio should be enough to restore equilibrium.[6]

What we can safely conclude based on the available research, as well as our experience as conflict coaches, is that we need to ensure we make *more than one* bid for repair for each rupture, with a 3:1 ratio the minimum, and 5:1 likely to achieve the best result. Regardless of the exact ratio you aim for, all available literature underscores the importance of maintaining a much higher volume of positive interactions over the negative in working relationships.

What counts as a bid for repair?

Bids for repair come in many forms and at different magnitudes. They include anything from a sincere, specific apology after a serious argument, to friendly eye contact or a genuine smile after a slightly brusque exchange of words. Each situation will require a different combination of bids for repair to achieve your 5:1 ratio.

Examples of categories for bids for repair are shown in Table 5.

What repair looks like in practice

The 5:1 ratio can sound overwhelming to start with – masterclass participants often say 'Do I really have to do *that much* after a disagreement?' – and at first it can seem hard to know what kind of repair is appropriate for the rupture you've experienced.

However, it's much more intuitive than it first sounds – you will already unconsciously be making bids for repair in your relationships all the time, you just may not think of them like that (yet!). And most bids for repair take moments, no more. These are some examples of what repair might look like in common scenarios. Do bear in mind that some bids for repair (e.g. compliments, invitations to drinks) may be interpreted differently depending on gender and culture, so do use your personal and professional judgement on what's appropriate in each case.

1) **You've had a tense exchange with Habiba, another member of the team on a decision you don't agree on. The decision hasn't gone your way, and there's no possibility of revisiting it, which you accept. You were both frustrated and expressed this. You are still feeling bruised by the conversation, and suspect she is too.**

   Bid 1: After letting 24 hours pass for you both to calm down, you send Habiba a message saying:

   > *'Hi Habiba, hope your day is going well. I found yesterday's conversation quite hard, and I think you might have done too. I just wanted to reach out to say I understand your position and I'm sorry if I came across as frustrated. Our working relationship is important to me, and I'd welcome the opportunity of a chat today or tomorrow to clear the air if you have time.'*

   Bid 2: Habiba accepts your invitation. During the conversation, you express your desire to get back on track, and your appreciation for Habiba as a colleague. She accepts this too, and you have a good, task-focused session to go over anything not resolved.

Table 5: Bids for repair

WORDS

- Apology - only if something to apologise for!
- Acknowledgement - e.g. warm greeting.
- Affirmation - e.g. sincere praise in the moment.
- Appreciation - for qualities you notice.
- Interest: 'How was...?' 'What do you think about...?'

GESTURES

- Proactive communication - checking in; thoughtful 'content'.
- Invite them to participate, even in small ways (input, meetings, events).
- Take an interest - as a person.
- Make them a coffee/buy them a drink/offer the biscuits!
- Signal warmth and liking - reassurance of 'we're OK'

Bid 3: When you see Habiba in the office you warmly greet her and ask her about her weekend, and spend some time chatting about life outside the office.

Bid 4: In the next meeting where you are together, you openly acknowledge a point Habiba makes which you find particularly insightful.

Bid 5: When you are going out to get coffee, you make a concerted effort to offer one to Habiba and bring back her exact order.

2) **You took the lead role on a team client presentation, which went well. James, who is at the same level of seniority but has less experience in that sector, feels he should have led the pitch and has told you he's unhappy at being given a less visible role, and feels pushed out by you.**

Bid 1: You tell James that it absolutely wasn't your intention to make him feel like that, and you are sorry it's had that impact on him, which you didn't anticipate. You ask if you can have a conversation so you can understand where he is coming from, and so you can explain your reasoning.

Bid 2: During that conversation you explain why you insisted on leading – which was due to being the only member of the team with the previous senior experience in the sector that the brief demanded. You ask James if there's a way he thinks it could have been handled differently, which would have felt more fair. You express to James your respect for him as a professional and a colleague, and suggest ways you could both go about debating the allocation of roles next time.

Bid 3: You invite James along to a networking event you are going to later that week, which will help him to build contacts in the industry.

Bid 4: You introduce James to an old work colleague of yours at the event, drawing attention to some of James' achievements in your introduction.

Bid 5: You invite James to grab a pizza on the way home from the event, and spend some time talking about work and life in a relaxed setting.

3) **After remaining calm following several similar incidents, you lose your temper and raise your voice at Martien, an admin assistant who is making repeated mistakes in correcting documents, which you feel is making you look incompetent to others. You have taken to double checking his work – time you do not have and you feel resentful for – but a major error has slipped through the net. You make it clear how angry you are that this has happened again. Martien is shocked, upset and apologetic. You leave the call abruptly, still irritated.**

Bid 1: After reflecting for a few hours, you realize that raising your voice was unacceptable and you feel regret at how you spoke to Martien, which was driven by both the frustration and resentment the situation has caused. You go to find Martien to apologize, and open with:

> *'I don't think I handled the situation this morning well, and I want to apologize for how I spoke to you. Our working relationship is important to me and I'd like to have a conversation so we can move forward. Are you open to that?'*

Bid 2: Martien would like to have a further conversation but asks if it can be tomorrow morning, as he is still reflecting on what happened. You agree on a time, and meet at 9am the next morning. You lead a task-focused conversation to explore what's going wrong in how the documents are handled and how mistakes can be eradicated, using the Hard Conversations Framework. You take a coaching approach to support Martien to identify solutions, and ask him to make some commitments on how he is going to do things differently from now on.

Bid 3: Later that day you send Martien a message to express your appreciation for his contributions to the meeting and his willingness to work with you on the solution.

Bid 4: The next document comes to you with zero errors. You immediately message Martien to acknowledge his effort in implementing the new process, and the change you've noticed.

Bid 5: During your next team call you chat with Martien as you both wait for the rest of the team to arrive, taking interest in the hobby you know is important to him and sharing some highlights of your progress on your own.

In all of these examples, it's clear that some concerted energy and clear intentions are needed to put the Five Rs of Smart Conflict into practice. Making a repair can take a conscious effort, and you can use the Five R model to triage where you need to pay the most attention in each case. Sometimes a more structured, thoughtful conversation is the first act of repair and *Readiness* is essential to success, as well as having a planned *Response* or two up your sleeve, along with some forms of words that allow you to express your desire to work it out and allow a *Repair* that create a seam of liquid gold in your relationship, rather than leaving a crack.

However, in most cases bids for repair are intuitive, quick, easy and require very little effort on your part. In the section on The Marble Jar below, we'll look at how we can develop a habit of making conscious 'bids for the relationship' with people we work with, especially in relationships which are – or have the potential to be – more difficult.

A note on apologies

'What we do after we hurt someone is as important as the hurt itself.' – Mary Ainsworth, *Patterns of Attachment*[7]

An apology goes a long way. But it has to be genuine. An insincere apology, also known as a non-apology, does more harm than good.

A genuine apology takes responsibility for the actions or behaviour that caused some kind of harm (personal or professional) or pain (emotional or physical) to the other person. By admitting or acknowledging our part in what happened and showing remorse, we can begin to rebuild trust and restore the relationship. Without this acknowledgement of responsibility, the apology fails to address the core issue and won't effectively repair the relationship. Non-apologies tend to prolong conflict and resentment, and often cause further frustration, reinforcing negative feelings and undermining the possibility of repair.

If your own apologies sound like versions of *'I'm sorry you feel that way'* or *'I apologize if you were offended'* pause here to return to the *Reflection* chapter to explore why you might find it difficult to take responsibility for your part in conflict situations. As always, have self-compassion – there are many reasons why we might resort to this kind of non-apology, the most common of which being we haven't experienced or witnessed many genuine apologies ourselves so we don't have a model for them. The good news is that like all of the techniques in this book, with practice you can learn to make genuine apologies which really do repair things.

If you are on the receiving end of a non-apology, try not to get frustrated, and pay attention to staying regulated if strong emotions come up, or pause the conversation if it feels like it might escalate. Like many scenarios when we aren't on the same page with someone at work, trying to get back to Task Conflict (the task being to understand what has happened and the impact) can be a strategy that opens up the possibility of real understanding and repair.

When we should apologize… and when we shouldn't

Put simply, we should apologize when we realize we have done something – intentionally or accidentally – that has upset or harmed someone else. In general, a sincere apology costs us nothing and solves much. Accidentally stepped on someone's foot in the bus queue? Apologize. Talked over your colleague in your enthusiasm to get your ideas out? Apologize. Realized you got too competitive with another candidate in the race for promotion? Apologize. Claimed someone else's work as your own? Apologize, and desist that idea-stealing behaviour immediately. Whether we have a close relationship with someone or not, whether we have to see them every day or will never encounter them again, part of being a decent human is having the humility to say sorry when we're in the wrong.

However, there are times when we might be tempted to apologize, even feeling an irresistible emotional drive to do so, but it's not smart. Some people identify strongly as people pleasers. People pleasing refers to a pattern of behaviour where individuals consistently prioritize others' needs and desires over their own, often to their detriment. People pleasing is closely related to the psychological construct of sociotropy 'characterized by an excessive investment in interpersonal relationships and a strong need for social acceptance',[8] which over time can lead to depression, anxiety and burnout through consistently putting your own needs at the bottom of the priority list. If you have a tendency to be people pleasing, you may reflexively apologize for things you really shouldn't apologize for.

Typical examples are: excessively apologizing for asking someone to complete a task which is unequivocally part of their job, therefore undermining your own professional authority; or apologizing for yourself when you make a very reasonable request and the other person responds rudely or inappropriately, signalling that you will accommodate their poor behaviour now, and in future. Prioritizing being liked by pleasing the other person over the more uncomfortable job of potentially displeasing them to get the right outcome is an understandable and very typical type of *Avoidance*. You might convince yourself that apologizing profusely and then exiting the chat or backing out of the room quickly is in service of the greater good, but often when we apologize to avoid a potentially harder conversation we are signalling to the other person that *we* are in the wrong, and willing to be walked over again next time, too.

If you know you have a tendency to over-apologize for fear of being disliked, or apologize when you objectively aren't in the wrong, head back to the *Response* chapter to find smarter strategies.

The relational marble jar

> *'Trust is built in very small moments. It's not a sweeping, dramatic gesture—it's a collection of small, meaningful actions over time. When someone remembers your dog's name, when they check in on you after a hard day, when they respect your boundaries—those are marbles in the jar. And when the jar is full, we feel safe, we feel seen, we feel like we can rely on that person. But trust can also be lost in an instant. A thoughtless betrayal, a broken promise, or consistent disengagement can empty the jar quickly. Trust is built slowly but lost fast.'*
>
> Brené Brown, *Rising Strong*

The concept of an 'emotional bank account', was first introduced by Stephen R. Covey in his now classic self-leadership book, *The 7 Habits of Highly Effective People*. Covey uses the bank account metaphor to describe the ebb and flow of trust and emotional investment in relationships, where positive actions are 'deposits' that build trust, and negative actions are 'withdrawals' that diminish it.[9] Brené Brown – best known as an academic researcher and author on the subjects of vulnerability, courage, shame and empathy – built on this concept, introducing the metaphor of the relational 'marble jar.'[10] In her book *Daring Greatly* she tells the story of her daughter's teacher, who used a marble jar to reward or remove marbles based on students' behaviours. We can think of each working relationship we are in as having its own marble jar, the contents of which are constantly fluctuating. Each positive interaction, such as keeping a promise, showing kindness or listening actively, adds a marble to the jar. Conversely, breaking trust – such as betraying a confidence or being dismissive – removes marbles. Over time, relationships with fuller marble jars (more trust) are stronger and more resilient, while those with fewer marbles are fragile and more likely to break under pressure.

It's not only when we've been involved in conflict or had to have a hard conversation that we need to think about our mutual marble jars. Investing in the relationship by adding positive marbles in our daily interactions is what will build the resilience of the relationship and make important conversations feel easier when you need to have them.

The power of filling an empty jar

This concept is almost embarrassingly simple, and although we have witnessed time and again how that simple shift can transform the way teams relate to one another, we used to feel a bit self-conscious about introducing it into workshops for our very 'serious' Board and Executive clients, especially in the more no-nonsense and conflict-prone sectors. However, time and again we've found it's the Marble Jar that changes everything, when we least expect it.

Steve, Chief Compliance Officer on the Executive Team of a pharmaceutical company we were team coaching, became a very unlikely evangelist for the idea of the relational marble jar. Steve had joined the company as a graduate and had never worked anywhere else. With a 20-year tenure under his belt, he was a trusted leader and part of a tight-knit inner circle of Executives who had been there from the start. The problem was that people outside that circle didn't like him very much. He was ruthlessly efficient but extremely abrasive. In pre-coaching interviews, his direct reports had described him as 'rude, arrogant, self-centred and egotistical.' Yikes.

As Leadership and Conflict coaches and educators on Smart Conflict, we are accustomed to clients and masterclass participants interrogating and pushing back on the ideas and interventions we introduce. It's part of the process of them becoming invested in the work, and making sense of it in their own context. It's also a demonstration of the exact kind of Task Conflict and healthy debate we advocate for. Frankly, we *love* it. There is nothing better. It keeps us on our toes as coaches, and this is often how the best learning takes place.

Figure 8: The Marble Jar

That said, Steve showed he was in a league of his own when it came to our session with the Executive Team on Smart Conflict. He could not stop interrupting, arguing with and countering the concepts we were introducing. He seemed entirely negative, incredulous at what we were suggesting, and a bit cross, for reasons that were hard to identify. While Q&A is often the most useful part of a workshop, Steve's dominance and continued interruptions were derailing the session and impacting the learning of the rest of the team. Louise – who was leading – took the decision to assertively but kindly shut Steve down. He was quiet and perfectly reasonable for the remainder of the workshop, but the experience was so stressful that afterwards Louise went into a side room and shed a few tears – both in relief that it had gone well in spite of the grilling she'd received, and in disappointment that Steve had turned out to be so combative and resistant to the work the team urgently needed to do to change some of their more damaging leadership behaviours.

But over the next few weeks, something unexpected happened. Steve's behaviour started to change – dramatically. Whereas before the session he was known for abruptly giving instructions to his team without so much as a 'hello,' and had shown little to no interest in them otherwise, he started enquiring about their weekends. And saying please, and thank you. And acknowledging when a job had been done well. He started offering to make rounds of tea now and again, to the disbelief of those who'd known him for 20 years and didn't think he even knew where the kitchen was. What on earth had happened? What soon became clear was that the concept of the relational bank account – and specifically The Marble Jar and how empty all of his must surely be – had struck Steve with such force he'd experienced one of those rare but transformational 'alarm clock moments' in his self-awareness. He'd had a clear vision of how others were seeing him, and he did not like what he saw.

Over the next months, the concept of 'putting marbles in the jar' became part of the whole Executive Team's language, and completely changed how they collectively thought about building trust – between themselves and with their own teams. In the post-coaching interviews Steve's direct reports remarked, with astonishment and genuine warmth, how much his behaviour had changed, and their gratitude for his efforts to be more engaged and appreciative. These efforts were sometimes awkward and clunky (old habits are hard to break), but this just seemed to endear him to them more. It was so clear he was *trying*, and that meant everything to them.

Another unexpected side effect of this behaviour change was that some time later Steve was promoted to one of the most senior C-Suite roles in the company. Before his discovery of The Marble Jar there had been concerns that Steve didn't have the interpersonal leadership skills such a pivotal role required, but his commitment to changing his previously gruff and command-and-control style pushed him over the line to achieve the promotion he'd been hoping for his whole career.

The repair conversation guide

There will be times when asking someone about their weekend or complimenting their new shoes will absolutely not cut it in terms of making a repair. When you've had a serious disagreement, argument or there has been another kind of major rupture between you and a colleague or client, a much more structured approach to repair is required.

Here we'll share with you a Repair Conversation guide that draws on the principles of mediation that you can use to get back on track with another, more constructive conversation. It's important to use language that feels natural to you, so practise how you might phrase each step in your own words. Don't skip steps or change the order, however – the most important part of the process is to identify where you *do* agree before getting into where you don't.

1) **Adopt a curious mindset to understand where they are coming from and give them your full focus**

   'I'd really like to understand what's happening from your perspective'

2) **Acknowledge you are not on the same page**

   'It's clear that we are not on the same page/have different perspectives/don't agree on this'

3) **Set out your desire to work it out**

   'I would really like to have a conversation to reach an understanding so we can move forward'

4) **Start with what you do agree on**

   'I think we can both agree that we would like to resolve this'

   'I think we can both agree we need to find a solution that works for everyone'

   'I think we can both agree we want what's best for the client/the team/the business'

   'I think we can both agree that Annabel was unhappy with the outcome of the meeting on Friday'

5) **Outline where you appear to disagree**

   'It seems we have reached different conclusions about the nature of the problem/whether there is a problem'

   'It seems we might have different ideas on how this should be handled'

   'It seems like although we are both trying to achieve the same thing for the client/the business/the team we have different perspectives on the way we do that/what professional communication looks like/how decisions should be made'

   'It seems like that although we both agree on the series of events on Friday, we have different perspectives about the impact they had and how we need to manage Annabel as the key stakeholder'

6) **Get curious to understand their perspective (explore the unmet needs, notice any false assumptions, as well as the presenting issue)**

   'How are you seeing it from your perspective? What do you need from me to feel better about it?'

7) **Summarize what you heard them say and check for understanding**

   'So if I have understood correctly you think/feel... Have I got that right?'

8) **Only now share your perspective speaking from 'I'**

   'So how I saw it was... which meant I felt... and so I concluded...'

9) **Identify possible solutions. Make and hear suggestions until something becomes agreeable to both of you**

   Don't be disheartened if you don't find immediate solutions. Time and reflection are a key part of getting to resolution. You may need to do this process over several meetings depending on how high feelings are running.

What if it can't be repaired?

Forgiveness is a wonderful thing, which can bring a great deal of peace to both giver and receiver. But it's not compulsory. There are some things that each of us finds unforgivable, and that boundary will vary (sometimes significantly) from person to person. We've witnessed teams who have had stand-up shouting matches involving offensive personal insults recover, forgive and go on to be more bonded and high performing than ever. And others where a war of attrition and underlying unpleasantness has led to an irrecoverable situation where one or more people felt the need to leave the team or the business entirely, due to the extent of damaged trust.

It's possible in many scenarios to carry on having a perfectly civil and functional relationship with someone at work without forgiving past hurt. But it is certainly harder, not least because of the emotional and mental bandwidth holding a grudge can take. So wherever possible, repair is the smart choice – resolving a conflict and letting it go gives you back the headspace for other, more productive, uses of your time.

If you feel like you are involved in a conflict that can't be repaired and you think you are past the point of no return, revisit *Reflection* and consider whether this conclusion is driven by one of your 'defaults'. Are you basing your conclusion on past experiences of conflicts that haven't been able to be resolved? Are you resorting to catastrophic thinking, without enough objective evidence on which to base your decision? Is there anything else you could try before accepting it can't be fixed and walking away, in one form or another?

In our experience, most conflicts at work *can* be repaired, even those that feel terminal at the time. If you would like to fix it, there's almost always a way. Have hope, and lean in for another try.

Repair summary

- **All meaningful relationships experience moments of rupture. It's not only large ruptures like arguments that matter, small moments of misunderstanding and misattunement can cause cracks in the relationship.**
- **It's important to make a conscious effort to repair a rupture if you want the relationship to continue.**
- **The ratio of rupture to repair is important: for every rupture you need 3 to 5 'bids for repair' to restore equilibrium.**
- **Apologies are an important tool for repair, but it's important to know when it's not smart to apologize and another strategy will be more effective.**
- **We have a relationship 'marble jar' with everyone we work with. We can make relationships more resilient to conflict by keeping the jar full, and replacing marbles lost through ruptures.**

10 Making it stick

'The secret of getting ahead is getting started.' – Mark Twain[1]

In this book we've tried to outline how hard conversations are the gateway to personal, team and organizational growth. And how every brave conversation forges better task outcomes, and deeper, more trusting relationships. We hope you can see that you don't have to choose one or the other. You can absolutely move towards both at the same time; they are truly interconnected. If you've made it this far, by now you've explored why hard conversations matter, how to approach them with the Smart Conflict Five R model and the Five-Step Hard Conversations Framework. And you will have started the work to rethink your default responses, and to upskill on how to navigate them more effectively. But reading a book and amassing knowledge alone isn't enough to drive new habits: the real challenge is turning the insight and good intentions into lasting behavioural change.

This final chapter is about making the change and making it stick. Our deeply ingrained, default habits – avoidance, defensiveness, over-explaining, shutting down – are wired into our brains, from many years of repetition. Rewiring the neural pathways that create our instinctive responses will take consistent effort, self-awareness, and deliberate practice. The good news is it is completely possible to rewrite our behaviours and habits thanks to what is known in neuroscience as neuroplasticity.

This chapter will show you how to develop habits that stick through small, sustainable changes that compound over time. If you commit to the process, change is inevitable.

The neuroscience of change

Neuroplasticity is the brain's ability to rewire itself by forming new neural connections in response to learning and practice. The more we repeat a behaviour, whether avoiding conflict or handling it well, the stronger the neural pathway becomes. You may have heard the expression '*Neurons that fire together, wire together*' meaning that when we practise something new, like pausing before reacting, or speaking from 'I' in hard conversations, these behaviours become more automatic and faster over time (in a process called myelination).[2] Helpfully, at the same time, our old habits weaken when they aren't reinforced by our behaviour.

The goal isn't to become flawless at hard conversations and handling conflict; it's to make progress. Some days, you'll navigate a tough conversation brilliantly. Other days, you'll catch yourself slipping into autopilot, and find you've thrown all your new learning out the window. Possibly literally. That's normal, and not a reason to give up. Change happens when we can tolerate the off days, identify and accept we've fallen off the wagon, and dust ourselves off and come back to the principles once again. We should very much expect to slip up, so we need a plan for when, not if that happens.

One thing we hope you've taken away from this book is that when it comes to our ability to master hard conversations, our talents are not fixed in stone. Everything you need boils down to a learnable skill. No one is born naturally good at hard conversations; people who handle them well have had some combination of good role models, put in the practice, taken time to reflect and accepted that with consistent effort they will improve over time.

Handling setbacks

No matter how much you prepare, and follow the models we've outlined in this book, not every hard conversation will go exactly as you want it to, and that's ok. It's an inevitably messy, trial-and-error process. Sometimes you'll think you couldn't have done more but the other person did not respond as you wanted. We have to accept that ultimately we cannot change and control other people or their behaviour. We can only influence it.

In his book *Learned Optimism*, Dr. Martin Seligman, a founder of positive psychology, defined the '3 Ps' – Personalization, Pervasiveness and Permanence – the three mindset traps we can fall into after setback:[3]

1) **Personalization** – '*This is all my fault*.'

   Replace '*I completely messed that up*' with '*That didn't go to plan, I'll own my part, but it's not all on me.*'

   Replace '*I made things worse.*' with '*Tension can be part of progress – this might be a step towards clarity.*'

2) **Pervasiveness** – '*This affects everything.*'

   Replace '*This one bad conversation proves I'm terrible at conflict.*' with '*Just because this one situation went badly doesn't mean I don't handle others well.*'

   Replace '*That was a disaster.*' with '*That was one data point.*'

3) **Permanence** – '*This will always be this way.*'

   Replace '*I'll never get better at this.*' with '*This is a skill, and I'll improve with practice.*'

   Replace '*That was a disaster.*' with '*I'm refining my approach with real-world practice.*'

Whatever the reason you feel there has been a setback, take a moment afterwards to reflect using these prompts:

1) What just happened?
2) How am I responding (my thoughts and feelings)?
3) Was this a one-off, or am I noticing a pattern in my responses to certain contexts?
4) What's my learning?
5) What if any new action will I take now/next time?

Building effective conflict habits

From goal setting to intention setting

You've probably set a million goals in your lifetime. You've probably reached some of them, forgotten about many of them and not achieved many more (not yet at least!). There's a lot to be said for setting goals, in particular to give clarity to what it is you're trying to get to, so you know where you are heading and when you have arrived. But goals alone aren't enough; the habits you implement are what will drive you towards your goals.

When it comes to hard conversations, those habits are probably going to be about swapping out a current response for a new one, and psychologist Peter Gollwitzer has a really easy and effective model to help you do just that – it's called *If-Then Planning*.[4]

In *If-Then Planning*, you need to anticipate the automatic behaviour you currently have which is getting in the way of you achieving your desired result, and swap it for a new planned response.

It looks like this:

If (trigger), then I will (new behaviour)

For example, *If I feel defensive in a tough conversation, then I will take a breath and ask a clarifying question before responding.*

What intentions do you need to set to achieve your conflict goals?

If...	*Then...*

There is a large evidence base proving that our environment has an outsized impact in shaping our behaviour, and our ability to form new habits and stick to them.[5] Changing your route to work so it does not involve passing the artisan coffee shop will make it a lot easier to spend less on coffee because you've removed it visibly from your environment and don't have to rely on (infamously weak) willpower. When it comes to hard conversations, changing our environment is not so easy – we can't simply start avoiding others, we need to take them on the journey with us.

It's true we can only control our own behaviour, but it's also true that culture change, within a team or an entire organization, is still *individual* change, just at scale. If you are looking to change how you show up in hard conversations at work, it's going to be a lot easier if your colleagues go on the journey with you and you re-engineer your conflict culture together. Creating a shared language and shared set of experiences that can be articulated in a Conflict Code or Behavioural Charter and embedded through daily rituals is one way that many of our clients have successfully supported such a cultural transformation.

Another habit hack is to embed your new behaviours into your existing routine. This means we rely less on the very unreliable and limited resource known as willpower, and instead use what B. J. Fogg calls 'habit anchoring.'[6] Habit anchoring is the act of pairing a new habit with something you already do regularly. So instead of trying to 'find time' to practise conflict skills, you are much more likely to succeed if you anchor a new habit onto existing ones. You can do this by thinking: after I do 'x.'... I will do 'y.'

For example:

> *'After I review my calendar each morning, I will prepare any key messages I need to land for any difficult conversations I need to have today.'*

> *'After 50 minutes in my 1:1 with my team member, I will ask if there's anything I could be doing differently to help them do their job better.'*

> *'After I take a deep breath before a tough conversation, I will remind myself to listen first, then respond.'*

1% better every day: The power of marginal gains

Another thing we know about successful habit creation is that if we set big audacious goals we are more likely to fail. Seems obvious, right? But for some reason we tend to do this anyway. Much better to accept that slow, steady, consistent progress, and aggregate marginal gains are more likely to deliver the big transformations we are looking for, albeit over a longer timeframe than perhaps we would ideally like. The 1% rule states that making small, consistent improvements every day leads to exponential change over time, and certainly worked well for Sir Dave Brailsford who used this principle to lead the British Cycling Team from mediocrity to Olympic Golds and beyond.[7] Don't aim for perfection right now, just aim to be slightly better today than you were yesterday, every day. You might choose one micro-practice to do each day. Perhaps tomorrow you are simply going to aim to ask more questions, and make fewer statements. And see what that reveals.

Embrace over-correction

When we learn a new skill, and try out new tools and techniques, it can take a while before using these new skills feels natural. Initially you are likely to feel very awkward and the work will feel laboured. Our clients often report feeling 'inauthentic' when trying out new behaviours and this makes perfect sense – the old you would not have shown up in this way! But change and new habit building requires you to put on a metaphorical new pair of shoes, which will be uncomfortable and stiff at first, until you wear them in and they too become part of your shape. If being authentically you today is not getting you the results you need, you need to be authentic about your intention and desire to grow and do things better.

The evidence base suggests that successful change is not just about what you do – it's about becoming who you want to be, and to make the leap we need to believe we can be a new version of us and borrow this future identity now.[8] For example, if you see yourself at an identity level as someone who struggles with conflict, you'll likely default to avoidant behaviours. But when you shift your identity, your actions start aligning with it. So instead of aligning yourself with an identity that says '*I'm no good at conflict*' you might choose to think instead '*I'm someone who has the conversations that matter*'. So in those inevitable moments when you feel like avoiding the conversation, if you tap into this new identity it takes the pressure off the thing you can't entirely control (how the conversation goes and the outcome) to reminding yourself that you are the sort of person that leans in and tries. This should make a real difference because you get to take an action that will reinforce your sense of this new self. And of course over time, the more you act in alignment with your new identity, the more natural it will become until this truly is effortlessly you.

Tell everyone your goal

A study by Dr. Gail Matthews from Dominican University concludes that when we speak our goals out loud to others and write down our plans, we increase the likelihood of following through by a significant 33%.[9] Tell your colleagues and your team about your intention to get better at hard conversations, and how you are going to do it. Tell them what they can expect from you moving forward and ask them to hold you to account on your promises. You might even inspire them to share their growth goals too.

Seeking and accepting feedback

Getting better at hard conversations can't just be measured by how you feel before, during and after them. If you are aiming to get better results from your hard conversations and build higher-performing teams through them, you are going to need your colleagues to let you know how they are experiencing you. Their feedback is critical data to make any blind spots visible.

Asking for feedback should be one of your new habits if you are serious about getting better at hard conversations. And once in a blue moon won't cut it. You need to create regular opportunities to keep you accountable and reinforce progress – remember you want to know when you are nailing it, not just when you are not, so you know which behaviours to double down on. This is really going to accelerate your growth.

Keep going

When all is said and done, just by reading this book you have taken the first step towards your goal of getting better at hard conversations. What you do next doesn't matter – just do something. More than 70% of you reading this won't take any action at all. Will you choose to be in the 30% who fully embrace a new identity as someone who has the conversations that matter at work and take action to make it happen?

Let's get started right now. What's one new habit you'll commit to starting today? Write it down here:

If…

Then I will…

Further resources

There are a number of further resources to support you in the real world as you begin your journey to implementing everything you have learned in this book and truly master Smart Conflict.

This includes the Smart Conflict Workbook which contains all the exercises outlined in the book.

You can access all the bonus materials here: www.thepowerhouse.company/resources

Smart Conflict style diagnostic

The questions contained in this diagnostic have been designed to help you identify your default conflict style, giving you a customized report for where to lean into this style, and the contexts where another style might be more effective.

Visit: www.thepowerhouse.company/diagnostics

Smart Conflict team scorecard

Understanding your baseline conflict competence as a team is an important step for teams and organizations looking to improve this vital leadership skill. This team diagnostic gives you a custom report showing how your team is performing against each of the Five Rs of Smart Conflict and specific suggestions on the key focus areas to improve your collective performance.

Visit: www.thepowerhouse.company/diagnostics
Here you can also find our 'Smart Conflict for Teams' Guide which walks you through how to apply many of the book's tools and techniques in team settings.

Smart Conflict keynotes, programmes and workshops

If you are looking for help to increase conflict competence in your team or organization, our Smart Conflict Talks, Programmes and Workshops have been designed to inspire your colleagues and support you all to successfully implement and embed the principles and practicalities of Smart Conflict in a sustainable and lasting way.

Visit: www.thepowerhouse.company/services

Resolve a conflict

To find our more about how Conflict Wayfinder offers an effective and structured solution for resolving existing conflicts between colleagues visit www.thepowerhouse.company/services

And finally... we want to hear from you

We would love nothing more than to hear your stories of real-life hard conversations you've leaned into after reading this book, and of course, how they went. Email us at hello@thepowerhouse.company

Acknowledgements

Many people expressed amazement that we'd decided to write this book alongside scaling The Power House, travelling around the country to deliver our demanding programme of masterclasses, running our busy coaching practice and juggling our respective young children and the competing demands of family life, and we did it the hard way, for sure. None of this would have been possible without our husbands – Ivo and Christian – who have, with extremely good grace, gone above and beyond to enable us to do what we needed to do to get everything over the line. Our enduring thanks to them both.

Our Smart Conflict methodology would not exist without our clients, from whom we have learned so much. The individuals who have shared their most vulnerable moments in coaching; the teams that invited us to share the very earliest iterations of our masterclass; and the organizations who have chosen us to deliver Smart Conflict education and training at scale. Over the months of writing the manuscript for this book we delivered corporate Hard Conversations training to thousands of managers, directors and partners, executive teams and boards across industries. Their excellent questions, challenge and engagement allowed us to continually refine our thinking, and their many success stories gave us the confidence we were really onto something.

Sincere thanks to all our beta readers, who gave their time to provide thoughtful feedback on the early draft: Eleanor Ford, Christina Patterson, Derek Hill, Paul Barbour, Amirali Sharifian, Samantha Farrell, Roselyn Xavier, and Ivo van Haarst. Thanks also to Christian Gill for the illustration, and to Sylvie van Haarst for all her inspiration on cover designs. And much gratitude to everyone at Practical Inspiration Publishing – particularly Alison and Shell – who provided both the support and the challenge we needed to stay on track. There are many others we can't begin to list here who have helped and encouraged us in so many ways – to all of you, our heartfelt appreciation.

Alice would like to thank her late mother, Elizabeth, for being a constant source of inspiration, and in particular for role-modeling that the identities of 'mother' and 'published author' can co-exist, and her father for his steadfast interest and belief in her work and for always encouraging her to take the moon shots. Louise would like to thank her mother, Lynda, always her greatest cheerleader and an impressive example of constant self-development; her late father, whose pride spurred her on; and The Hags, for being there.

Importantly, we want to thank each other. While we threw ourselves into the process of writing this book with enormous enthusiasm, being a first-time author and writing with another extremely smart woman who is also your co-founder was always fraught with potential danger. However, it has left us even more grateful for our partnership and with greater admiration for our complementary skillsets. And yes, there were times when we had to take our own medicine and use Smart Conflict techniques in the more pressurized moments. And reader, it works.

Notes

Introduction

[1] Eurich, Tasha. *Insight*. MacMillan, 2017.

[2] Commonly attributed to Dorothy Thompson, though the original source remains unverified.

[3] Jehn, K. A., F. R. C. de Wit, and L. Greer. 'The Paradox of Intragroup Conflict: A Meta-Analysis.' *Journal of Applied Psychology*, vol. 97, no. 2, 2012, pp. 360–390.

[4] Advisory, Conciliation and Arbitration Service (Acas). 'Acas Annual Report and Accounts, 2021 to 2022 (web-optimised PDF).' Acas, 14 July 2022.

[5] Society for Human Resource Management (SHRM). 'SHRM Civility Index Q1 2025.' SHRM, March 2025.

[6] Tjosvold, Dean. 'The Conflict-positive Organization: It Depends Upon Us.' *Journal of Organizational Behavior*, vol. 29, no. 1, 2007, pp. 19–28.

[7] Cortina, Lilia M., et al. 'Incivility in the Workplace: Incidence and Impact.' *Journal of Occupational Health Psychology*, vol. 6, no. 1, 2001, pp. 64–80.

[8] De Dreu, Carsten K. W., and Laurie R. Weingart. 'Task versus Relationship Conflict, Team Performance, and Team Member Satisfaction: A Meta-Analysis.' *Journal of Applied Psychology*, vol. 88, no. 4, 2003, pp. 741–749.

[9] Sterud, Tom, and Therese N. Hanvold. 'Effects of Adverse Social Behaviour at the Workplace on Subsequent Mental Distress: A 3-year Prospective Study of the General Working Population in Norway.' *International Archives of Occupational and Environmental Health*, vol. 94, no. 2, 2020, pp. 325–334.

[10] Castellini, Giovanna, et al. 'Conflicts in the Workplace, Negative Acts and Health Consequences: Evidence From a Clinical Evaluation.' *Industrial Health*, vol. 61, no. 1, 2022, pp. 40–55.

[11] Cambridge Dictionary. 'conflict' | Meaning in the Cambridge English Dictionary', dictionary.cambridge.org/dictionary/english/conflict Accessed 3 April 2025.
[12] Edmondson, Amy C. *The Fearless Organization: Creating Psychological Safety in the Workplace for Learning, Innovation, and Growth*. John Wiley & Sons, 2018.

What is Smart Conflict?

[1] Jehn, Karen A. 'A Multimethod Examination of the Benefits and Detriments of Intragroup Conflict.' *Administrative Science Quarterly*, vol. 40, no. 2, 1995, pp. 256–282.
[2] Neff, Kristin D. 'Self-Compassion: An Alternative Conceptualization of a Healthy Attitude Toward Oneself.' *Self and Identity*, vol. 2, no. 2, 2003, pp. 85–101.
[3] Aronson, Elliot, and Philip Worchel. 'Similarity Versus Liking as Determinants of Interpersonal Attractiveness.' *Psychonomic Science*, vol. 5, no. 4, April 1966, pp. 157–158.
[4] Rogers, Carl. *On Becoming a Person*. 1961.
[5] Tronick, E., et al. 'The Infant's Response to Entrapment between Contradictory Messages in Face-to-Face Interaction.' *Journal of the American Academy of Child Psychiatry*, vol. 17, no. 1, 1978, pp. 1–13.
[6] Gottman, John, et al. *What Makes Love Last? How to Build Trust and Avoid Betrayal*. Simon & Schuster, 2013.

Why we fear conflict in life and work

[1] Deci, Edward L., and Richard M. Ryan. 'The "What" and "Why" of Goal Pursuits: Human Needs and the Self-Determination of Behavior.' *Psychological Inquiry*, vol. 11, no. 4, 2000, pp. 227–268.
[2] Ware, Bronnie. *The Top Five Regrets of the Dying: A Life Transformed by the Dearly Departing*. Hay House, Inc, 2012.
[3] Holt-Lunstad, J., et al. 'Loneliness and Social Isolation as Risk Factors for Mortality: A Meta-Analytic Review.' *Perspectives on Psychological Science*, vol. 10, no. 2, 2015, pp. 227–237.
[4] Redcay, Elizabeth, et al. 'Live Face-to-face Interaction During fMRI: A New Tool for Social Cognitive Neuroscience.' *NeuroImage*, vol. 50, no. 4, 2010, pp. 1639–1647.
[5] Tjosvold, Deon, and Haifa F. Sun. 'Understanding Conflict Avoidance: Relationship, Motivations, Actions, and Consequences.' *International Journal of Conflict Management*, vol. 13, no. 2, 2002, pp. 142–164.
[6] Kross, Ethan, et al. 'Social Rejection Shares Somatosensory Representations With Physical Pain.' *Proceedings of the National Academy of Sciences*, vol. 108, no. 15, 2011, pp. 6270–6275.

[7] Rosenberg, Morris, and Nevitt Sanford. 'Self and Society: Social Change and Individual Development.' *American Sociological Review*, vol. 31, no. 5, 1966, pp. 746–747.
[8] Deci, Edward L., and Richard M. Ryan. *Intrinsic Motivation and Self-Determination in Human Behavior*. Springer eBooks, 1985.
[9] Cloud, Henry. *Boundaries for Leaders: Results, Relationships, and Being Ridiculously in Charge*. Harper Business, 2013.

The influence of genetics, family, culture and gender

[1] Locke, John. *Some Thoughts Concerning Education*, 1693.
[2] Bowlby, J. 'Attachment and Loss. Vol. I.' *Mental Health (London)*, vol. 28, 1969, p. 28.
[3] Ainsworth, Mary D. Salter, et al. *Patterns of Attachment: A Psychological Study of the Strange Situation*. Lawrence Erlbaum Associates, 1978.
[4] Berisha, Gentrit, Besnik Krasniqi, and Rrezon Lajçi. 'Birth Order Revelations about Managers.' *Management Research Review*, vol. 45, no. 10, 2022, pp. 1249–1274.
[5] Doidge, Norman. *The Brain that Changes Itself: Stories of Personal Triumph from the Frontiers of Brain Science*. Penguin UK, 2008; Doidge, Norman, M.D. *The Brain's Way of Healing: Remarkable Discoveries and Recoveries from the Frontiers of Neuroplasticity*. Scribe Publications, 2015.
[6] Frazzetto, Giovanni, et al. 'Early Trauma and Increased Risk for Physical Aggression During Adulthood: The Moderating Role of MAOA Genotype.' *PLOS One*, vol. 2, no. 5, 2007, e486; Hettema, John M., Michael C. Neale, and Kenneth S. Kendler. 'A Review and Meta-Analysis of the Genetic Epidemiology of Anxiety Disorders.' *American Journal of Psychiatry*, vol. 158, no. 10, 2001, pp. 1568–1578. https://doi.org/10.1176/appi.ajp.158.10.1568; Turkheimer, Eric, and Mary Waldron. 'Nonshared Environment: A Theoretical, Methodological, and Quantitative Review.' *Psychological Bulletin*, vol. 126, no. 1, 2000, pp. 78–108; Jang, Kerry L., W. John Livesley, and Philip A. Vemon. 'Heritability of the Big Five Personality Dimensions and Their Facets: A Twin Study.' *Journal of Personality*, vol. 64, no. 3, 1996, pp. 577–591.
[7] de Waal, Frans. *The Age of Empathy: Nature's Lessons for a Kinder Society*. Crown, 2008.
[8] Sternberg, Robert J., and Lawrence J. Soriano. 'Styles of Conflict Resolution.' *Journal of Personality and Social Psychology*, vol. 47, no. 1, 1984, pp. 115–126. https://doi.org/10.1037/0022-3514.47.1.115
[9] World Health Organization. *World Report on Disability*. 2011. www.who.int/publications/i/item/9789241564182 Accessed 10 April 2025.
[10] American Psychiatric Association. *Diagnostic and Statistical Manual of Mental Disorders: DSM-5* (5th ed.), 2013; Milton, Damian E. M. 'On the Ontological

Status of Autism: The "Double Empathy Problem"'. *Disability & Society*, vol. 27, no. 6, 2012, pp. 883–887.

[11] Barkley, Russell A. *Taking Charge of ADHD: The Complete, Authoritative Guide for Parents*. 3rd ed., The Guilford Press, 2013; Martel, Michelle M., and Joel T. Nigg. 'Child ADHD and Personality/Temperament Traits of Reactive and Effortful Control, Resiliency, and Emotionality'. *Journal of Child Psychology and Psychiatry*, vol. 47, no. 11, 2006, pp. 1175–1183. https://doi.org/10.1111/j.1469-7610.2006.01629.x; Barkley, Russell A., and Mariellen Fischer. 'The Unique Contribution of Emotional Impulsiveness to Impairment in Major Life Activities in Hyperactive Children as Adults'. *Journal of the American Academy of Child and Adolescent Psychiatry*, vol. 49, no. 5, 2010, pp. 503–513. https://doi.org/10.1097/00004583-201005000-00011; Shaywitz, Sally E. *Overcoming Dyslexia: A New and Complete Science-Based Program for Reading Problems at Any Level*. Alfred A. Knopf, 2003; Carroll, Julia M., and Margaret J. Snowling. 'Language and Phonological Skills in Children at High Risk of Reading Difficulties'. *Journal of Child Psychology and Psychiatry*, vol. 45, no. 3, 2004, pp. 631–640. https://doi.org/10.1111/j.1469-7610.2004.00252.x; Cermak, Sharon A., and Dawne Larkin. *Developmental Coordination Disorder*. Delmar Cengage Learning, 2002.

[12] Meyer, Erin. *The Culture Map: Breaking Through the Invisible Boundaries of Global Business*. PublicAffairs, 2014.

[13] Eagly, Alice H., and Steven J. Karau. 'Role Congruity Theory of Prejudice Toward Female Leaders'. *Psychological Review*, vol. 109, no. 3, 2002, pp. 573–598; Varghese, Lebena, Meghan I. Huntoon, and Lisa Finkelstein. 'Dodging the double bind: the role of warmth and competence on the relationship between interview communication styles and perceptions of women's hirability'. *European Journal of Work and Organizational Psychology*, vol. 27, no. 4, 2018, pp. 1–12.

[14] Helgesen, Sally, and Marshall Goldsmith. *How Women Rise: Break the 12 Habits Holding You Back from Your Next Raise, Promotion, or Job*. Legacy Lit, 2018.

[15] Holt, Jennifer L., and Cynthia James DeVore. 'Culture, Gender, Organizational Role, and Styles of Conflict Resolution: A Meta-analysis'. *International Journal of Intercultural Relations*, vol. 29, no. 2, 2005, pp. 165–196.

[16] Bear, Julia, et al. 'Can Avoiding Conflict Be Beneficial? A Field Investigation of Gender, Conflict Avoidance, Emotional Labor, and Emotional Exhaustion' IACM 2011 Istanbul Conference Paper. June 2011. SSRN Electronic Journal. https://ssrn.com/abstract=1866524

Reflection

[1] Attributed to Carl Jung.

[2] 'Self-Awareness'. Encyclopedia.com. www.encyclopedia.com/humanities/dictionaries-thesauruses-pictures-and-press-releases/self-awareness Accessed 8 April 2025.

[3] Kilmann, Ralph. *Mastering the Thomas-Kilmann Conflict Mode Instrument: Celebrating More Than 50 Years of Resolving All Kinds of Conflicts*. Kilmann Diagnostics, 2023.

[4] Ainsworth, Mary D. Salter, et al. *Patterns of Attachment: A Psychological Study of the Strange Situation*. Lawrence Erlbaum Associates, 1978.

[5] Karpman, Stephen B. 'Fairy Tales and Script Drama Analysis.' *Transactional Analysis Bulletin*, vol. 7, no. 26, 1968, pp. 39–43. http://karpmandramatriangle.com/pdf/DramaTriangle.pdf

[6] Berne, Eric. *Games People Play: The Psychology of Human Relationships*. Grove Press, 1964.

[7] Emerald, David. *The Power of TED: The Empowerment Dynamic*. Polaris Publishing, 2005.

[8] Maister, David H., Charles H. Green, and Robert M. Galford. *The Trusted Advisor*. Free Press, 2000.

[9] Bailey, R. and Jose Pico. 'Defense Mechanisms.' *StatPearls*. Edited by Maribeth Villegas, StatPearls Publishing, 2023. www.ncbi.nlm.nih.gov/books/NBK559106/ Accessed 10 April 2025.

[10] Doidge, Norman. *The Brain That Changes Itself: Stories of Personal Triumph from the Frontiers of Brain Science*. Penguin UK, 2008.

Regulation

[1] Frankl, Viktor E. *Man's Search for Meaning*. Translated by Ilse Lasch, Beacon Press, 2006. Note: The cited quote is widely attributed to Frankl, though it does not appear verbatim in this text.

[2] Cannon, Walter B. *Bodily Changes in Pain, Hunger, Fear and Rage: An Account of Recent Research into the Function of Emotional Excitement*. D. Appleton and Company, 1915.

[3] Taylor, Shelley E., et al. 'Biobehavioral Responses to Stress in Females: Tend-and-befriend, Not Fight-or-flight.' *Psychological Review*, vol. 107, no. 3, 2000, pp. 411–429.

[4] Levine, Peter A. *In an Unspoken Voice: How the Body Releases Trauma and Restores Goodness*. North Atlantic Books, 2010.

[5] Carter, C. Sue. 'Neuroendocrine Perspectives on Social Attachment and Love.' *Psychoneuroendocrinology*, vol. 23, no. 8, 1998, pp. 779–818.

[6] Hayes, Steven. *A Liberated Mind: The Essential Guide to ACT*. Vermilion, 2019.

[7] Nedergaard, Johanne S. K., and Gary Lupyan. 'Not Everybody Has an Inner Voice: Behavioral Consequences of Anendophasia.' *Psychological Science*, vol. 35, no. 7, 2024.

[8] Harris, Russ. *The Happiness Trap 2nd Edition: Stop Struggling, Start Living*. Hachette UK, 2022.

[9] 'Dr. Russ Harris – Acceptance Commitment Therapy.' *YouTube*. www.youtube.com/@dr.russharris-acceptanceco972

[10] Neff, Kristin D. 'Self-Compassion: An Alternative Conceptualization of a Healthy Attitude Toward Oneself.' *Self and Identity*, vol. 2, no. 2, 2003, pp. 85–101.
[11] Balban, Melis Yilmaz, et al. 'Brief Structured Respiration Practices Enhance Mood and Reduce Physiological Arousal.' *Cell Reports Medicine*, vol. 4, no. 1, 2023, pp. 100–895.
[12] Weaver, Libby. *Rushing Woman's Syndrome: The Impact of a Never-Ending To-Do List and How to Stay Healthy in Today's Busy World*. Hay House UK, 2017.
[13] Huberman, Andrew. 'The Physiological Sigh.' *Huberman Lab AI*, 2024. https://ai.hubermanlab.com/s/cCSj1L7a Accessed 10 April 2025.
[14] Johnson, Blair T., et al. 'Mental and Physical Health Impacts of Mindfulness Training for College Undergraduates: A Systematic Review and Meta-Analysis of Randomized Controlled Trials.' *Mindfulness*, vol. 14, no. 9, 2023, pp. 1–20.
[15] Kabat-Zinn, Jon. *Wherever You Go, There You Are: Mindfulness Meditation in Everyday Life*. Hachette Books, 2005.

Readiness

[1] Eisenhower, Dwight D. As quoted in: *Eisenhower: Soldier and President*, by Stephen E. Ambrose, Simon & Schuster, 1990.
[2] Rogers, Carl. *On Becoming a Person*, 1961.
[3] Landhuis, Esther. 'Brain Waves Synchronize When People Interact.' *Scientific American*, 1 July 2023. www.scientificamerican.com/article/brain-waves-synchronize-when-people-interact/
[4] Gilbert, Daniel T., and Timothy D. Wilson. 'Miswanting: Some Problems in the Forecasting of Future Affective States.' *Feeling and Thinking: The Role of Affect in Social Cognition*, edited by Joseph P. Forgas, Cambridge University Press, 2000, pp. 178–197.
[5] Wilson, Timothy D., and Daniel T. Gilbert. 'Affective Forecasting.' *Advances in Experimental Social Psychology*, vol. 35, 2003, pp. 345–411.
[6] Baumeister, Roy F., et al. 'Bad Is Stronger than Good.' *Review of General Psychology*, vol. 5, no. 4, 2001, pp. 323–370, doi:10.1037/1089-2680.5.4.323
[7] Torabizadeh, Camellia PhD, et al. 'Effects of the Problem Solving Technique in Type 2 Diabetic Patients with Cognitive Impairment: A Randomized Clinical Trial.' *International Journal of Community Based Nursing and Midwifery*, vol. 6, no. 3, 2018, pp. 197–208.
[8] Hadlaczky, Gergö, Emma Eliasson, Sara Sutori, et al. 'Systematic Review and Meta-Analysis: Effectiveness of Stand-Alone Digital Suicide Preventive Interventions for the Self-Management of Suicidality.' *Journal of Technology in Behavioral Science*, vol. 9, no. 3, 2023, pp. 440–451.
[9] Jeffers, Susan. *Feel the Fear and Do It Anyway*. Ballantine Books, 1987.

[10] Milad, Mohammed R., and Gregory J. Quirk. 'Fear Extinction as a Model for Translational Neuroscience: Ten Years of Progress.' *Annual Review of Psychology*, vol. 63, 2012, pp. 129–151.
[11] Grant, Adam. *Think Again: The Power of Knowing What You Don't Know*. Viking, 2021.
[12] Kruger, Justin, and David Dunning. 'Unskilled and Unaware of It: How Difficulties in Recognizing One's Own Incompetence Lead to Inflated Self-Assessments.' *Journal of Personality and Social Psychology*, vol. 77, no. 6, 1999, pp. 1121–1134.
[13] Sanford, Nevitt. *Where Colleges Fail: A Study of the Student as a Person*. Jossey-Bass, 1967.
[14] Shaw, George Bernard. *Attributed.*
[15] Weitzel, Sloan R. *Feedback That Works: How to Build and Deliver Your Message, First Edition*. Center for Creative Leadership, 2018.
[16] Goldsmith, Marshall, and Mark Reiter. *What Got You Here Won't Get You There*. 2011; Goldsmith, Marshall. 'Feedforward: Coaching for Behavioral Change.' *YouTube*, 26 August 2014. www.youtube.com/watch?v=BlVZiZob37I
[17] Deci, Edward L., and Richard M. Ryan. 'The "What" and "Why" of Goal Pursuits: Human Needs and the Self-Determination of Behavior.' *Psychological Inquiry*, vol. 11, no. 4, 2000, pp. 227–268.
[18] Tong, Stephanie T., and Joseph B. Walther. 'Relational Maintenance and CMC.' *Computer-Mediated Communication in Personal Relationships*, edited by Kevin B. Wright and Lynne M. Webb, Peter Lang, 2011, pp. 98–118.
[19] Dindo, Lilian, et al. 'Acceptance and Commitment Therapy: A Transdiagnostic Behavioral Intervention for Mental Health and Medical Conditions.' *Neurotherapeutics: The Journal of the American Society for Experimental NeuroTherapeutics*, vol. 14, no. 3, 2017, pp. 546–553.
[20] Rosenberg, Marshall B. *Nonviolent Communication: A Language of Life*. PuddleDancer Press, 2003.
[21] Vezich, I. Stephanie, et al. 'Modulating the Neural Bases of Persuasion: Why/How, Gain/Loss, and Users/Non-Users.' *Social Cognitive and Affective Neuroscience*, vol. 12, no. 2, 2017, pp. 283–297.
[22] Tversky, Amos, and Daniel Kahneman. 'Loss Aversion in Riskless Choice: A Reference-Dependent Model.' *The Quarterly Journal of Economics*, vol. 106, no. 4, 1991, pp. 1039–1061.
[23] Gnepp, Jackie, et al. 'The Future of Feedback: Motivating Performance Improvement through Future-Focused Feedback.' *PLOS One*, vol. 15, no. 6, 2020; Goller, Daniel, and Maximilian Späth. '"Good Job!"' the Impact of Positive and Negative Feedback on Performance.' *Sports Economics Review*, vol. 8, no. 2, 2024, p. 100045, doi:10.1016/j.serev.2024.100045
[24] Goldsmith, Marshall. 'Ten Surefire Reasons to Try Feedforward!' *MGSCC Knowledge Bank*. https://knowledgebank.mgscc.net/17-ten-surefire-reasons-to-try-feedforward/

Response

[1] This quote is widely attributed to Winston Churchill, though no definitive original source has been confirmed.
[2] Widdowson, Lucy, and Paul J. Barbour. *Building Top Performing Teams: A Practical Guide to Team Coaching to Improve Collaboration and Drive Organizational Success.* Kogan Page, 2021.
[3] Goleman, Daniel. *Emotional Intelligence: Why It Can Matter More Than IQ*. 1996.
[4] Bungay Stanier, Michael. *The Coaching Habit: Say Less, Ask More & Change the Way You Lead Forever*. Box of Crayons Press, 2016.
[5] Voss, Chris, and Tahl Raz. *Never Split the Difference: Negotiating as if Your Life Depended on It*. 2016.
[6] Holiday, Ryan. *The Obstacle Is the Way: The Timeless Art of Turning Trials into Triumph*. Portfolio, 2014.

Repair

[1] Commonly attributed to Jalāl ad-Dīn Muhammad Rūmī, though the original source remains unverified.
[2] Gottman, John M., and Nan Silver. *The Seven Principles for Making Marriage Work: A Practical Guide from the Country's Foremost Relationship Expert*. Harmony Books, 2015.
[3] Gold, Claudia M., and Ed Tronick. *The Power of Discord: Why the Ups and Downs of Relationships Are the Secret to Building Intimacy, Resilience, and Trust*. Little, Brown Spark, 2020.
[4] Gottman, John M. *The Science of Trust: Emotional Attunement for Couples*. W. W. Norton & Co, 2011.
[5] Losada, Marcial, and Emily Heaphy. 'The Role of Positivity and Connectivity in the Performance of Business Teams: A Nonlinear Dynamics Model.' *American Behavioral Scientist*, vol. 47, no. 6, 2004, pp. 740–765, doi:10.1177/0002764203260208
[6] Fredrickson, Barbara L., and Marcial F. Losada. 'Positive Affect and the Complex Dynamics of Human Flourishing.' *American Psychologist*, vol. 60, no. 7, 2005, pp. 678–686, doi:10.1037/0003-066x.60.7.678
[7] Ainsworth, Mary D. Salter, et al. *Patterns of Attachment: A Psychological Study of the Strange Situation*. Lawrence Erlbaum Associates, 1978.
[8] Sato, Toru, and Doug McCann. 'Sociotropy–autonomy and Interpersonal Problems.' *Depression and Anxiety*, vol. 24, no. 3, 2006, pp. 153–162.
[9] Covey, Stephen R. *The 7 Habits of Highly Effective People: Powerful Lessons in Personal Change*. Simon & Schuster, 2004.
[10] Brown, Brené. *Daring Greatly: How the Courage to Be Vulnerable Transforms the Way We Live, Love, Parent and Lead*. Penguin, 2015.

Making it stick

[1] Twain, Mark. *Attributed.*

[2] Paus, Tomás. 'Mapping Brain Maturation and Cognitive Development During Adolescence.' *Trends in Cognitive Sciences*, vol. 9, no. 2, 2005, pp. 60–68; Gogtay, Nitin, Jay N. Giedd, L. Lusk, et al. 'Dynamic Mapping of Human Cortical Development During Childhood Through Early Adulthood.' *Proceedings of the National Academy of Sciences*, vol. 101, no. 21, 2004, pp. 8174–8179.

[3] Seligman, Martin E. P. *Learned Optimism: How to Change Your Mind and Your Life*. Alfred A. Knopf, 1991.

[4] Gollwitzer, Peter M. 'Implementation Intentions: Strong Effects of Simple Plans.' *American Psychologist*, vol. 54, no. 7, 1999, pp. 493–503.

[5] Wood, Wendy, and David T. Neal. 'A New Look at Habits and the Habit–Goal Interface.' *Psychological Review*, vol. 114, no. 4, 2007, pp. 843–863.

[6] Fogg, B. J. *Tiny Habits: The Small Changes That Change Everything*. Houghton Mifflin Harcourt, 2020.

[7] London Business Forum. 'Sir Dave Brailsford – the 1% Factor.' *YouTube*, 1 December 2016. www.youtube.com/watch?v=NQxYlu12ji8

[8] Verplanken, Bas, and Jie Sui. 'Habit and Identity: Behavioral, Cognitive, Affective, and Motivational Facets of an Integrated Self.' *Frontiers in Psychology*, vol. 10, 2019, p. 1504.

[9] Matthews, Gail. 'The Impact of Commitment, Accountability, and Written Goals on Goal Achievement', *Psychology Faculty Presentations*, no. 3, 2007, Dominican University of California. https://scholar.dominican.edu/psychology-faculty-conference-presentations/3/

Bibliography

Introduction

Edmondson, Amy C. *The Fearless Organization: Creating Psychological Safety in the Workplace for Learning, Innovation, and Growth*. John Wiley & Sons, 2018.

Eurich, Tasha. *Insight: The Power of Self-Awareness in a Self-Deluded World.* MacMillan, 2017.

Gottman, John, and Nan Silver. *What Makes Love Last? How to Build Trust and Avoid Betrayal*. Simon & Schuster, 2013.

Rogers, Carl. *On Becoming a Person*. 1961.

Part 1: Understanding conflict at work

Why we fear conflict in life and work

Cloud, Henry. *Boundaries for Leaders: Results, Relationships, and Being Ridiculously in Charge*. Harper Business, 2013.

Deci, Edward L., and Richard M. Ryan. *Intrinsic Motivation and Self-Determination in Human Behavior*. Springer eBooks, 1985.

Ware, Bronnie. *The Top Five Regrets of the Dying: A Life Transformed by the Dearly Departing*. Hay House Inc, 2012.

The influence of genetics, family, culture and gender

Ainsworth, Mary D. Salter, et al. *Patterns of Attachment: A Psychological Study of the Strange Situation*. Lawrence Erlbaum Associates, 1978.

Barkley, Russell A. *Taking Charge of ADHD: The Complete, Authoritative Guide for Parents*. 3rd ed., The Guilford Press, 2013.

Bates, Laura. *Fix The System, Not the Women*. Simon & Schuster, 2023.

de Waal, Frans. *The Age of Empathy: Nature's Lessons for a Kinder Society*. Crown, 2009.

Doidge, Norman. *The Brain that Changes Itself: Stories of Personal Triumph from the Frontiers of Brain Science*. Penguin UK, 2008.

Doidge, Norman, M.D. *The Brain's Way of Healing: Remarkable Discoveries and Recoveries from the Frontiers of Neuroplasticity*. Scribe Publications, 2015.

Folger, Joseph P., Marshall Scott Poole, and Randall K. Stutman. *Working Through Conflict: Strategies for Relationships, Groups, and Organizations*. 9th ed., Routledge, 2021.

Helgesen, Sally, and Marshall Goldsmith. *How Women Rise: Break the 12 Habits Holding You Back from Your Next Raise, Promotion, or Job*. Legacy Lit, 2018.

Meyer, Erin. *The Culture Map: Breaking Through the Invisible Boundaries of Global Business*. PublicAffairs, 2014.

Shaywitz, Sally E. *Overcoming Dyslexia: A New and Complete Science-Based Program for Reading Problems at Any Level*. Alfred A. Knopf, 2003.

Part 2: The Smart Conflict Five R model

Reflection

Berne, Eric. *Games People Play: The Psychology of Human Relationships*. Grove Press, 1964.

Emerald, David. *The Power of TED: The Empowerment Dynamic*. Polaris Publishing, 2005.

Karpman, Stephen B. *A Game Free Life*. Drama Triangle Publications, 2014.

Karpman, Stephen B. *Collected Papers in Transactional Analysis, Volume 1*. Drama Triangle Publications, 2019.

Kilmann, Ralph. *Mastering the Thomas-Kilmann Conflict Mode Instrument*. Kilmann Diagnostics, 2023.

Maister, David H., Charles H. Green, and Robert M. Galford. *The Trusted Advisor*. Free Press, 2000.

Regulation

Cannon, Walter B. *Bodily Changes in Pain, Hunger, Fear and Rage: An Account of Recent Researches into the Function of Emotional Excitement*. D. Appleton and Company, 1915.

Frankl, Viktor E. *Man's Search for Meaning*. Translated by Ilse Lasch, Beacon Press, 2006.

Goleman, Daniel, and Richard J. Davidson. *Altered Traits: Science Reveals How Meditation Changes Your Mind, Brain, and Body*. Penguin, 2018.

Harris, Russ. *The Happiness Trap 2nd Edition: Stop Struggling, Start Living*. Hachette UK, 2022.

Hayes, Steven. *A Liberated Mind: The Essential Guide to ACT*. Vermilion, 2019.

Kabat-Zinn, Jon. *Wherever You Go, There You Are: Mindfulness Meditation in Everyday Life*. Hachette Books, 2005.

LeDoux, Joseph. *Anxious: Using the Brain to Understand and Treat Fear and Anxiety*. Penguin, 2016.

Levine, Peter A. *In an Unspoken Voice: How the Body Releases Trauma and Restores Goodness*. North Atlantic Books, 2010.

Neff, Kristin. *Self-Compassion: The Proven Power of Being Kind to Yourself*. William Morrow, 2011.

Peters, Steve. *The Chimp Paradox: The Acclaimed Mind Management Programme to Help You Achieve Success, Confidence and Happiness*. Random House, 2015.

Weaver, Libby. *Rushing Woman's Syndrome: The Impact of a Never-Ending To-Do List and How to Stay Healthy in Today's Busy World*. Hay House UK, 2017.

Readiness

Goldsmith, Marshall, and Mark Reiter. *What Got You Here Won't Get You There*. 2011.

Grant, Adam. *Think Again: The Power of Knowing What You Don't Know*. Viking, 2021.

Jeffers, Susan. *Feel the Fear and Do It Anyway*. Ballantine Books, 1987.

Kahneman, Daniel. *Thinking, Fast and Slow*. Farrar, Straus and Giroux, 2011. Chapter 26, 'Prospect Theory,' explains loss aversion in depth.

Rogers, Carl. *On Becoming a Person*. 1961.

Rosenberg, Marshall B. *Nonviolent Communication: A Language of Life*. PuddleDancer Press, 2003.

Sanford, Nevitt. *Where Colleges Fail: A Study of the Student as a Person*. Jossey-Bass, 1967.

Weitzel, Sloan R. *Feedback That Works: How to Build and Deliver Your Message, First Edition*. Center for Creative Leadership, 2018.

The 'being' of readiness – mindsets and tools for overcoming blocks

Dweck, Carol. *Mindset: Changing the Way You Think to Fulfil Your Potential*. Robinson, 2017.

Eurich, Tasha. *Insight: The Power of Self-Awareness in a Self-Deluded World*. Macmillan, 2017.

Response

Bungay Stanier, Michael. *The Coaching Habit: Say Less, Ask More & Change the Way You Lead Forever*. Box of Crayons Press, 2016.

Goleman, Daniel. *Emotional Intelligence: Why It Can Matter More Than IQ*. 1996, ci.nii.ac.jp/ncid/BA28658620

Holiday, Ryan. *The Obstacle Is the Way: The Timeless Art of Turning Trials into Triumph*. Portfolio, 2014.

Locke, John. *Some Thoughts Concerning Education*. 1693.

Voss, Chris, and Tahl Raz. *Never Split the Difference: Negotiating as if Your Life Depended on It*. 2016.

Widdowson, Lucy, and Paul J. Barbour. *Building Top Performing Teams: A Practical Guide to Team Coaching to Improve Collaboration and Drive Organizational Success*. Kogan Page, 2021.

Repair

Ainsworth, Mary D. Salter, et al. *Patterns of Attachment: A Psychological Study of the Strange Situation*. Lawrence Erlbaum Associates, 1978.

Brown, Brené. *Daring Greatly: How the Courage to Be Vulnerable Transforms the Way We Live, Love, Parent and Lead*. Penguin, 2015.

Covey, Stephen R. *The 7 Habits of Highly Effective People: Powerful Lessons in Personal Change*. Simon & Schuster, 2004.

Gold, Claudia M., and Ed Tronick. *The Power of Discord: Why the Ups and Downs of Relationships Are the Secret to Building Intimacy, Resilience, and Trust*. Little, Brown Spark, 2020.

Gottman, John M. *The Science of Trust: Emotional Attunement For Couples*. W. W. Norton & Co, 2011.

Gottman, John M., and Nan Silver. *The Seven Principles for Making Marriage Work: A Practical Guide from the Country's Foremost Relationship Expert*. Harmony Books, 2015.

Making it stick

Clear, James. *Atomic Habits: An Easy & Proven Way to Build Good Habits & Break Bad Ones*. Random House Business, 2018.

Edmondson, Amy C. *The Fearless Organization: Creating Psychological Safety in the Workplace for Learning, Innovation, and Growth*. John Wiley & Sons, 2018.

Fogg, B. J. *Tiny Habits: The Small Changes That Change Everything*. Houghton Mifflin Harcourt, 2020.

Seligman, Martin E. P. *Learned Optimism: How to Change Your Mind and Your Life*. Alfred A. Knopf, 1991.

Index

Page numbers in *italics* and **bold** denote figures and tables, respectively.

www.ingramcontent.com/pod-product-compliance
Lightning Source LLC
LaVergne TN
LVHW091127080826
845145LV00008B/2068